AF609729

The Softness of Water

A collection of stories inspired by the Tao Te Ching, and other treasures of eastern philosophy

by Rebecca Beattie

Copyright Notice

Copyright © Rebecca Beattie 2010

The author asserts the moral right to be identified as the author of this work.

All Rights Reserved. No part of this publication may be reproduced, stored in any retrieval system, or transmitted in any form or by any means, electronic, mechanical, photocopying, recording or otherwise, without the prior permission of the author. Any unauthorised broadcasting, public performance, copying or re-recording will constitute an infringement of copyright.

This book is sold subject to the condition that it shall not, by way of trade or otherwise, be lent, re-sold, hired out or otherwise circulated without the author's prior consent in any form of binding or cover other than that in which it is published and without a similar condition including this condition being imposed on the subsequent purchase.

First published in Great Britain 2012

ISBN 978-1-291-16983-6

Contents

The Little Rabbit Who Thought Too Much

A long time ago, in a land not so very far away from here, lived two rabbits in a little house in the corner of a large green field. "Two rabbits living in a house?" I hear you say. "How absurd!" But it is true! The two rabbits lived very happily together, one little black rabbit and one little white rabbit.

The white rabbit was a very careful little rabbit. Whenever she had a task to do, she liked to think it all through from beginning to end, to make sure that she did everything just right and didn't get any surprises along the way. Her room was very tidy and all her things were put neatly away in all the right places. If you ever had to ask the white rabbit if she could lend you something, she would always know exactly where to find it. Her books were all neatly arranged from A to Z, and her clothes were all neatly arranged in tidy little piles or hanging in the wardrobe according to colour.

The black rabbit on the other hand was a little messier than this, and she loved surprises. Whenever she had a task to do, she would dive in head first, like a kingfisher into a pool, swim about a bit and then think about what it was she was meant to do. The black rabbit's room was very untidy, and also very colourful. She had different coloured clothes hanging all over the place, and her books were found in little piles all round the room. If you ever needed to borrow something from the little black rabbit, it might take her ages to remember where she had seen it last.

One day the two little rabbits decided to take a day away from their usual hopping about the field, nibbling on grass, so that they could get themselves ready for the year ahead. It was a beautiful spring day, the weather was dry and sunny, and so they decided to make a list of all the jobs they needed to do that day.

"Paint the fence, plant the vegetable garden, nibble the lawn..." said the white rabbit, writing the list of tasks on a large piece of paper. "What else?"

"Clean the windows and weed the flower beds," said the black rabbit.

"Gosh! We have got a lot to do. Where shall we start?" said the white rabbit. "Well, I suppose we could start by splitting the list of jobs down the middle and take half each. That might work... or maybe it would be better if we worked together on each task, that way we can complete each one in half the time. Oh, I don't know..." she scratched her ears as she thought about it. "Shall we have a cup of dandelion tea and think about it?"

"Oh, ok," said the black rabbit who knew very well what was coming next.

She knew the little white rabbit was very good at procrastinating, and could go on thinking about it all day long if she wasn't careful, and they would get to the end of the day having not completed a single task. She sighed, and slipped out of the back door and into the garden, whilst the white rabbit chattered away to herself in the kitchen as she put on the kettle, and looked in the cupboard for two cups that were just the right colour and the same size.

The black rabbit looked around the garden and breathed in a deep lungful of air. What a beautiful day, and how lovely to feel so purposeful. She knew she would enjoy today. As she began to look round the garden, she spotted a few weeds poking out from the flower beds, in between the beautiful roses that were just beginning to come into bud. She hopped over to them, and started to pull them out, careful to make sure she pulled all the roots out, so they didn't grow back too quickly. She could hear the sounds of the little white rabbit making tea in the kitchen, and thought to herself,

"Oh well, I may as well pull a few more weeds out while I am waiting for the tea,", and so she did.

"Tea's ready!" called the white rabbit, as she came into the garden a few minutes later carrying two steaming (and perfectly matched) mugs.

"I'll be there in a moment," said the black rabbit, tugging on a particularly stubborn dandelion root. "There, that's it!" she said, satisfied with the little pile of weeds beside her.

"Oh, you've finished!" said the white rabbit.

"Oh yes! So I have!" said the black rabbit with some surprise as she looked at the now-tidy and weed free flower beds. "What's next?"

"Well, we still have the vegetable patch to plant. Why don't we start there?" said the white rabbit, sipping her tea delicately.

When they had finished their tea, they made their way over to the vegetable patch, where the recently turned earth was all ready to be planted.

"Right, well... would you like to start with the carrots or the lettuce first?" asked the white rabbit.

"Oh, I don't mind," said the black rabbit, picking up the first packet of seeds from the pile, and making her way over to the far end of the vegetable patch.

"Right then," said the white rabbit, "I'll start with the carrots. Should I plant them in straight lines? And if so, which direction should I go in?"

As she stopped and thought about this, she glanced over at the black rabbit, who was by now halfway along her second row of lettuce seeds, humming away to herself quite happily.

“Right well, I suppose straight lines it is,” decided the white rabbit, and carefully started to measure out and dig holes in the cool damp earth to put the seeds into.

By the time she had measured and planted her sixth seed, the black rabbit stood up on her hind legs and brushed the soil off her front paws.

“Well, I am done,” she said. “Shall I start on the next job?”

And so it continued for the next few hours, with the black rabbit very purposefully working her way through the list, humming away to herself quite happily, while the white rabbit sat and thought a lot about what they needed to do before carefully starting each task, or sometimes never even getting to start, as by the time she had finished thinking about it and was ready to start, the black rabbit had already finished the job.

By the time it got to tea time, there was just one more task to do – they had to paint the fence. Whilst the white rabbit was still finishing off washing her last few windows, the black rabbit got all of the pots of paint out of the shed, and found all the brushes and cleaned them ready for the task ahead. If they could work quickly, they should be able to get one coat of paint on the fence done before it got too dark, and then they could finish off tomorrow morning. The black rabbit glanced over at the white rabbit and saw that the white rabbit still hadn’t finished, and she was standing looking at her last window with a thoughtful look on her face, so the black rabbit went into the kitchen and made them both some sandwiches and lemonade. Then she sat in a garden chair enjoying the last bit of afternoon sun while she ate her sandwich.

Once she had finished, she got up and decided to start work on the fence. By now, the white rabbit had at last finished her windows and came over to join the black rabbit.

“Well, which part of the fence should we start on do you think? Shall we start with this part here or that part over there?”

The little black rabbit sighed to herself, and picked up the paintbrush.

Later that night, an hour after it got dark, the little black rabbit looked out of her bedroom window. The full moon was sitting high in the night sky, lighting up the garden below her window.

“Hello?” called the black rabbit out of the window. “Are you alright out there? How can you see to paint in the dark? Don’t you think it would be better to come inside now and finish the painting tomorrow?

“That is probably a good idea,” said the voice from the darkened garden. “I will just think about that for a moment while I...” the white rabbit’s voice tailed off as she paused to think about it.

The black rabbit sighed again, and picked up her steaming mug of hot chocolate and her book, and got ready to settle in for a good night's sleep.

"Balance your thoughts with action. If you spend too much time thinking about a thing, you'll never get it done."

Bruce Lee

Pedro the Inventor

There was once a busy little honey bee called Gilbert who lived in a hive with lots of other busy little honey bees. Each morning he would wake up, stretch his six legs and his wings, yawn and prepare to fly out from the hive in search of fresh nectar to bring home for the honey. He would joyfully fly to the fields around his home-hive, and race towards the tall pink foxgloves that grew in high summer. There he would fall into each flower, and blissfully roll around, foraging and collecting the nectar, and once he had gathered almost more than he could manage in one trip, he would return to the hive and deposit it into the next part of the comb the bees were building that week.

Then he would fly further afield, to the purple heather that bobbed its head in the sunshine over the hill, and bumble his way round the golden gorse that smelled so beautifully of far off places.

Life for Gilbert was very happy. He had everything he wanted – a plentiful supply of nectar and honey, lots of work to do, and a queen bee watching over him that all the worker bees loved.

Gilbert's best friend was a worker bee called Pedro, who lived in the hive just a few cells away from Gilbert. Pedro's life was busy and filled with work too, but Pedro was discontented with his life and wanted it to change. Each morning he would wake up early, stretch out his six legs and his wings, and feel grumpy at the thought of all the work ahead of him that day. First he would have to follow the long line of other worker bees into the part of the hive where the eggs were kept, and then he would have to help tend the eggs so that they safely hatched and brought the next generation of bees to the hive. When they moved the eggs, the load felt heavy, the work was dangerous, and keeping the right temperature for the eggs was complicated. Occasionally when the beekeeper came to get the honey and draw the comb, a worker bee or two would get squashed. When they had finished looking after the eggs, the worker bees would then have to clean the cells, which were messy, and Pedro didn't like it at all.

Once he had finished his work, Pedro would feel exhausted, but always their queen would be issuing more orders to work harder or tunnel faster and bring back more food to the nest. When he saw his queen approaching to inspect the troops, he would groan inwardly and try and make himself invisible (which he mostly was to the queen) in case she or any of her generals saw him and found fault with him.

In the evenings, Pedro and Gilbert would meet together under the stars and talk about their day. Gilbert would leave the hive openly and tell the other bees where he was going, but Pedro somehow felt he would have to sneak out of the hive by a disused service tunnel that the rest of the hive had forgotten about.

Pedro and Gilbert would perch side by side on a wide leaf that hung over the damp grass and talk about what they had been doing that day and what they had seen and heard. Gilbert would generally be full of enthusiasm for the day he had had, and all the beautiful flowers he had bumbled around in his search for nectar, while Pedro would often be gloomy in his descriptions of his day, and the amount of hard work he had had to do. Pedro was generally frustrated by the lack of control he had in his life, and would often talk of how he would organise things if he was in charge, while Gilbert was a little more philosophical about things.

Pedro always thought that things would be run much better than they were now, if someone had put him in charge. Gilbert would listen quietly, knowing there was no point in questioning Pedro too closely; it didn't matter what the situation was or the circumstances, Gilbert knew that Pedro would have better ideas, and better ways of doing things, better ways of organising the Hive, and even the neighbouring ant hill when he really got going on his ideas.

"Well, I think we should do away having a queen bee, and have me in charge instead. I could organise things much better."

Gilbert smiled peacefully to himself, knowing that this was very unlikely, and also knowing that Pedro liked to express his opinions, but the chances were, if anyone did put Pedro in charge, he would not know where to start. Gilbert knew things worked perfectly well as they were. Nature was the best inventor there ever was, and ever since the great Queen of Every Hive had created the sky and the earth and the flowers, no one would ever be able to design things better.

"And another thing," said Pedro, who had continued talking himself into a frenzy all the time that Gilbert had been happy thinking and humming away to himself quietly. "I think I could show the rest of the honey bees a thing or two as well. The way you gather nectar is all very well, but if you put me in charge I could show you much better ways of selecting nectar, and then I am sure I could improve the formula of the honey. And another thing, I bet I could improve on some of the flower designs too."

At this point, Gilbert raised an antenna in surprise.

"Improve on flower designs?" he said. "Whatever do you mean? Flowers are perfect just as they are. How could you improve on something the Queen of Every Hive has created?"

"The great Queen of Every Hive?" Pedro snorted. "How can you be so childish Gilbert? Every bee knows that the world wasn't really created in a day by the Queen of Every Hive. That was just a story they told you when you hatched out of your egg. I bet I could have told you a better story, and I bet I could have created a better world too!"

This was too much even for Gilbert to digest, so he soon said goodnight to Pedro, and flew back to the hive, turning over all the things that Pedro had said in his mind. Pedro's ideas had confused him, and given him a feeling of anxiety in his stomach. Improve on nature? How was that possible? And the great Queen Bee of Every Hive didn't really create the world and the flowers and the hives and the honey? How was that possible? How had he got it all wrong, he wondered? What if he was wrong? How could he have thought the world was perfect all this time, if Pedro the worker bee could see its imperfections?

Gilbert felt most distressed and lay down to sleep, feeling very uneasy. All through the night, Gilbert kept waking up with a start, feeling very afraid, but he could not tell quite what he was afraid of exactly.

The next morning, he felt sluggish and tired and struggled to find anything that resembled his usually cheerful enthusiasm for his work. Somehow the colours on the flowers seemed dull, the scents that had been so delicious and enticing before now seemed quite ordinary. He couldn't quite work out why the world looked different this morning, all he knew was that it did. His thoughts still raced and he was most distracted. His day seemed to go really slowly, and he realised he was frowning. When one of the other bees saw him returning with the latest load of nectar to the comb, and asked him how he was, as he didn't seem to be his usual cheery self, he snapped a reply and felt quite grumpy.

"Don't seem myself?" he muttered, as he went back to work. "Oh, the nerve of it!"

Meanwhile, Pedro was busy at work, and feeling as resentful as ever. Today he felt oppressed by being one of hundreds of other worker bees, and he was sure life would be much better if he lived differently. He couldn't decide which he would prefer to be – either a King Bee, or a solitary bee, living alone and surviving on his wits in the great outside. He imagined striking out on his own and living by himself. How peaceful it would be and how wonderful to get up each day and please himself, instead of taking orders all the time.

When the bee in charge came round to check on the other worker bees' work, and make sure things were going according to schedule, Pedro became even more frustrated than before, and defiant and disrespectful of the bee in charge.

"You there, worker bee! Pedro isn't it? Get back in line and join in with your colleagues. How do you expect to get the comb ready if you are out of formation?"

"Out of formation?" Pedro muttered, a little too loudly under his breath. "Chance would be a fine thing. Life would be much better if I really was out of formation."

But he hadn't realised that the bee in charge was standing right behind him now, and had heard every word of his rude muttering. Nor did he realise that the bee in charge had been watching him for some weeks as he had thought Pedro was beginning to cause problems amongst the other bees. Dissent can be absorbed even through the pores of the skin, and unhappiness and dissatisfaction tend to be more catching than the strongest 'flu virus.

"Right, Pedro" shouted the bee in charge. "You are out of line. If you think you can do better on your own, then off you go. You can leave the Hive right now and see just how clever you are on your own!"

At the sound of all the shouting, all the other workers stopped what they were doing and turned around to see what was happening, but rather than feel embarrassed, this just made Pedro more defiant and belligerent. He held his head high, and slowly made his way out of the Hive, never once looking back.

"You are just stupid bees," he said loudly over his shoulder. "I will show you. I will show every bee… I can do much better on my own, without silly bees telling me what to do all the time. You wait and see. I will do just fine on my own."

In fact, Pedro was concentrating so hard on making his dramatic exit that he forgot to stop and get any of his things. The bee in charge sent one of the other workers to pack up Pedro's things into a little suitcase, and as Pedro was sitting outside the Hive wondering where to go, a suitcase of his things was very unceremoniously thrown out of the Hive. It bounced several times on the ground, and then landed with a thump at his six feet, and the catch broke, sending his belongings flying in all directions.

"The boss says you are not to come back until you have learned some sense," shouted the worker bee who had thrown the suitcase. "See ya, wouldn't want to be ya!" shouted the other bee with a laugh, and slammed the door of the Hive with a bang.

Pedro started to gather up his belongings, as it slowly dawned on him what had happened. He felt quite scared, but also quite exhilarated. He wasn't quite sure what to do or where to go, so he decided to go and sit on a leaf and wait for Gilbert to come, but Gilbert was still busy gathering nectar, and it was several hours before he came to meet Pedro, who was by then very bored and a bit grumpy from having had to wait for so long. Rather than triumphantly telling Gilbert what had happened while Gilbert admired Pedro for his bravery and cleverness as he had pictured it in his head, Gilbert listened quietly to Pedro's story and then gave a heavy sigh. Pedro was a little shocked and very disappointed with this reaction.

"Is that it? No 'congratulations, I knew you could do it'?" asked Pedro, incredulously.

Gilbert yawned sleepily, which only served to infuriate Pedro all the more. Pedro was so angry; he failed to notice that Gilbert was not his usual buzzy self. Instead, he just ranted a little more, and then got up and stormed off.

Gilbert yawned again, far too dejected to really notice Pedro's temper tantrum. He stretched his wings and decided to head home for the night. As Pedro got some distance from the leaf, his anger cooled and he realised he didn't actually have anywhere to go; it was as if someone had pulled the plug and all his energy and enthusiasm for his adventure drained away too. He couldn't go back to the Hive, as all the other bees would laugh at him. Instead he sat beneath a leaf and tried to get some sleep, but the air felt cold and the ground felt hard, and sleep didn't seem to want to come and cuddle up to him. So Pedro spent a very cold, miserable and lonely night out alone in the open air.

The next morning, as the sun rose in the pink sky, Pedro awoke from his all too brief sleep, and moaned to himself. All six legs felt stiff and aching, and when he stretched, he could hear his exoskeleton cracking.

"Nature," he said to himself, "is lumpy, bumpy and very uncomfortable. Now, if I was in charge, I would make it much more soft and comfortable."

As if in answer to his complaint, a large drop of rain fell out of the sky and knocked him off his six feet. He picked himself back up from the ground, and retreated under a leafy bush to wait out the storm. It was damp and it was cold, but at least it kept the worst of the rain off him.

Meanwhile, Gilbert had woken up after a more restful night than Pedro's. He had decided to go and seek some advice from one of the wise older bees who was so clever that he acted as an advisor to the queen. The old bee was called Jeremiah, and he had lived in the hive longer than most old bees' memories could remember. The young bee tapped on Jeremiah's door.

"Enter," a low voice came from inside, and as the little bee peered inside the chamber, he could just make out Jeremiah in the half-golden light, poring over an old book that was filled with strange symbols that Gilbert could not quite make out.

"Ah, there you are," said Jeremiah. "I was expecting you, young Gilbert."

"Really?" asked Gilbert, wondering how Jeremiah could have possibly known he was coming. "How did you know?"

"A simple deduction really," said Jeremiah. "Don't worry, I didn't foresee it in the nectar or read it in the thickness of the wax we have been producing of late. Usually you are a very buzzy, happy little fellow, but for the last day or so you have been grumpy and unhappy looking. What is troubling you?"

"Well, that is just it," said Gilbert. "I don't really know. I had a conversation with my friend about the Queen of Every Hive, and ever since then, I can't seem to shake off my bad mood."

Gilbert then relayed the contents of his conversation with Pedro to Jeremiah, and the old bee listened carefully.

"So," said Jeremiah, when Gilbert had finished, "Pedro questioned whether or not the Queen of Every Hive exists or not, and that has upset you? That is understandable really, as that is the world you were brought up in, and Pedro has questioned whether it is real or not."

"So, is he right? Is it just a story? Does the Queen of Every Hive really exist?"

"Well, what do you think?" asked Jeremiah.

"I don't know any more. I thought I did, but now I just want to know the truth, whatever that is." Gilbert's head drooped as he thought about it. "Does she exist, Jeremiah?"

"I don't know," said the old bee. "But does it matter what I know? Everyone's version of "truth" is different, because you can only experience truth in your own heart and mind, and each bee's heart and mind is different to the next. Someone once told me that you don't believe in the Queen of Every Hive, you experience her, in the flowers and the nectar and all of nature around us."

"Aha," said Gilbert, brightening a little. "Well, those things are definitely there, so maybe she is too."

"But tell me, Gilbert," said Jeremiah, "Does it matter what other bees believe? How does that change you?"

This question really confused Gilbert, and he shrugged, lost for words.

"What has changed in the world between the time that Pedro said those things to you, and the time before he said those things?"

"Hmmm… only my view of the world, I suppose."

"Absolutely," said Jeremiah. "The only thing that changed was your perception. So really, it doesn't really matter whether the Queen of Every Hive exists or not; it is your perception of whether she exists or not that matters. In life the only thing you can change is not other people's behaviour or beliefs, but your perception of those things. That can make the difference between a world where only cold and bad things exist, and a world you can live in and love."

Gilbert felt quite overwhelmed with all this information, but when he checked inside, the anxious feeling in his stomach had gone. He left Jeremiah then, and went back to work, feeling happier again and more like himself, his thoughts buzzing.

Meanwhile, Pedro had decided he was going to show every bee just what he could do when he was given the chance. He would show them that if they put him in control, he would show them how he could make a flower far more beautiful than anything Nature could do. This, he was sure, would prove that he was the best and cleverest bee there ever was.

"So," said Pedro to himself, "What would the most beautiful flower there ever was be like?"

He decided that the most beautiful stem was that of the foxglove, long and slender and graceful. But the foxglove was very high, and very heavy, and he would never be able to carry one by himself, so he decided instead to build his flower onto a foxglove stem that was already standing by the hedge, swaying gently in the breeze. He climbed high up onto the stem, and decided to remove the foxglove petals one by one to make way for his more beautiful petals. But when he got to the flowers, he couldn't help thinking how beautiful some of them were, so he left a few in place, and thought he would add some more colour to make it even more beautiful than the pinky-purple of the foxglove.

He decided that he liked the golden colour of the calendula flowers, and also the deep blue of the sweet pea. Which would it be? Pedro couldn't decide, so he thought that instead he would add all of them. But then the next problem came… how to attach them? He remembered then that he had a little ball of beeswax in his suitcase; that would be just the thing!

Pedro worked all day on his creation, carrying each petal to the flower and painstakingly attaching it with a little blob of beeswax. He also wanted his creation to smell nice. His favourite scent was of the golden flowers that grew amongst the sharp thorns on the gorse bush, as it smelled of faraway places that he had never seen. By the end of the day he had decided that if he mashed up the gorse petals and rubbed the mixture all over his creation, he should be able to get the lovely smell into his flower, so that evening, he rubbed gorse blossoms all over it. Then, exhausted, he curled up beneath his flower to sleep.

The next morning Pedro slept very late indeed. The sun was already high in the sky when he awoke, as he had worn himself out with all his hard work the night before. Pedro awoke with a jolt, remembering the wonderful creation he had made, and he jumped up to go and admire its beauty once more. He made his way to a spot a little distance away from the flower so he could look back and admire it. He was absolutely certain it would easily rival anything Nature could have created all on her own.

He took a deep breath, and turned around... and there it was. A tall graceful stem, that had bent slightly from the weight of all the beeswax, petals that had wilted or fallen off when the early morning sun rose and melted the beeswax, and smears of ugly yellow-brown mush where Pedro had rubbed on the gorse blossom. Nasty looking flies were buzzing all around it, and as Pedro stood and watched, he realised all the forager bees that were out gathering nectar that morning were keeping a clear distance away from it. They stopped at every single flower but this one, and when they saw it, they looked alarmed and flew away.

Pedro stared in horror at the ugly thing that stood before him, quite ruined, before going away to sit quietly alone and ponder his foolish pride and deciding what to say to the bee in charge when he returned to his Hive that evening, feeling very much more humble.

"You think you can take over the universe and improve it?

I do not believe it can be done.

Everything under heaven is a sacred vessel and cannot be controlled.

Trying to control leads to ruin.

Trying to grasp we lose.

Allow your life to unfold naturally.

Know that it is a vessel of perfection."

29th Verse of the Tao Te Ching, by Lao Tzu

"You are not in charge; you never have been and never will be."

Albert Einstein, Scientist.

The Bird and the Cobra

Long long ago, in a land of shifting sands amidst a beautiful river delta that ambled its way through the desert, there lived a little bird who spent his days flying through the clear, clean air with his flock. They would soar high into the deep blue sky, and travel up and down the banks of the river, which laid a narrow strip of green besides the blue, carried on streams of warm air.

When the sun sank beneath the Western hills, the little bird would roost with his flock amongst the columns and statues of old temples, which stood in their colourful glory on the Eastern Bank of the river. Many years before, great men had built these shining temples, chiselling the granite and sandstone by hand, one piece at a time, and then they had painstakingly carved and painted images of their world on the temple walls. The men were now long gone, and while the temples had crumbled and faded they still stood beneath the hot summer sun, where groups of people would gaze up at the walls in awe at what their ancestors had created, barely noticing the little flock of birds, who now made the temple their home.

Life for the flock of birds had a comfortable familiarity to it. Each day they would fly from the safety of their nests to the river a short distance away, where they would bathe and cool themselves in the shallow waters on the river banks, dig for fat worms in the fertile earth that lay beside it, and then fly back to the temples, in search of crumbs dropped by the visitors, or of insects flying through the air. As the sun reached its zenith at midday, they would seek shelter from its glare beneath the cool, shadowed walls until evening, when they would fly over the town in search of another meal. They rarely interacted with anyone not of their kind, always anxious not to become someone else's dinner.

As the night crept over the Western hills and threw its cool cloak over the land, the birds would roost together on top of the temple columns, in the gaps between the walls and the now largely absent ceiling, safe in the knowledge that the night hid them from sight of anyone, and they were high enough to be protected from anything slinking in the shadows on the ground below.

But after a time, the little bird began to wonder what lay beyond the Western hills, and he longed to find out. Surely there would be some adventure there? Unknown lands to explore meant there could be treasures beyond anything his imagination could give him, worms fatter than ever before, and insects bigger and juicier than the ones they knew here. Perhaps he might journey there, and learn things that none of the flock knew, then he could come home and they would all think that he was immensely clever and brave, and long to be like him. In truth the little bird knew he was the smallest of his flock, and he longed to be bigger and better than the others; he wished they would look at him with admiration shining in their eyes, instead of the protective and indulgent love that any group can sometimes grow for the smallest of their clan.

He always wondered what lay beyond the hills, but whenever he asked the older birds, they would simply tell him that there was nothing there he could want to see, or that it was just sand and rocks, or that he really didn't want to go there, before turning their attention elsewhere and leaving him wondering even more. He began to suspect that something mysterious lay beyond the hills that no one wanted to share with him. What was the secret they were keeping from him?

When he couldn't contain his curiosity any longer, he slipped away early one morning before the rest of the flock had stirred in their nests, before the sun began to rise and send its light into the darkest corners of their temple. Away he flew, over the town and its sleeping inhabitants, flying over the great river and on towards the hills and the big mountain that stood at the head of a deep valley.

By the time he had reached the mountain, he began to feel tired and hungry, and decided to land in search of some breakfast, eagerly anticipating the fat worms and juicy insects he had been imagining for so many months now. He landed on the rocky ground below, and although he searched and searched, he couldn't find any of the nice plump insects he usually ate, in fact he couldn't find anything at all besides the sand and the rocks, and the deep warmth of the sun, which was now creeping over the mountain and making the ground already too hot to stand on comfortably. He began to feel disheartened. Perhaps the other birds were right, and there wasn't anything here that was worth coming to see. He thought fondly of the river delta, and began to feel a little bit foolish.

But then a little distance away from him, he noticed something was moving, and looked over to see a cobra, sliding its way amongst the rocks and the sand, and the little scrubby plants that grew from time to time amidst the stones. Perhaps the cobra would tell him where he could find some nice breakfast, or some adventure?

"Excuse me," chirped the little bird to the cobra, "can you tell me where I might be able to find some breakfast? I have flown a long way, and I can't seem to find any insects or worms."

"Breakfassst?" hissed the cobra, sizing up the little bird with her two black bead-like eyes, "breakfassst. Hmmm, what a good idea!"

The cobra gently slid closer to the little bird, slowly, so that she would not alarm him and send him flying away. "I think you will find it isss far too hot and dry here to find any wormsss or insectsss."

As she spoke her little forked tongue slithered out from between her lips, and she hissed her words slightly. The little bird was fascinated by her, as he had never spoken with a cobra before, and felt quite grown up to be in a strange place having a conversation with a real life cobra. He remembered that the older birds had warned him never to stray too far on his own but he liked this feeling of adventure, as it made him feel cleverer. How impressed the other birds would be when he returned home and told them of his exciting day. The cobra hissed gently, and his attention turned again to her face, which seemed to have come closer to him while he was thinking about the rest of the flock, without him even noticing. Again, the cobra spoke,

"I know of a hole in the ground, not far from here where I think we might find some breakfassst," she hissed, thinking of her warm nest in the ground where her eggs lay, waiting to hatch. "It is cooler underground, and I am sure we can find something juicy and fat to eat there."

But the little bird was not quite as naive as the cobra had hoped, and he saw something deep in the eyes of the cobra that made him feel uneasy. In fact, he felt so alarmed by what he saw, that he spread his wings and jumped into the air, just as the cobra lunged at him, baring her fangs and shooting a spray of poison as she opened her mouth to eat him. He just about escaped without losing a single ruffled feather, but as he flew away into the blue sky that was covered with fluffy white clouds, he felt shaken, realising how close he had come to disaster.

He thought about his flock back amongst the temple walls, and worried about what to tell them, feeling foolish that he had not listened to their earlier advice, realising now that they had been wise to tell him there was nothing he wanted to see beyond the Western hills. But if he told them about his meeting with the cobra, they would know he had flown beyond the valley, even though they had told him not to, and that might get him into trouble. So he decided to tell the other birds nothing, and flew back to the flock and told them he had been flying over the town since before dawn, merely watching the people and the animals as they went about their daily business. The other birds said very little in response, and if they didn't believe his story, they certainly didn't tell him that.

But the image of the glint in the cobra's eye as she sized him up for breakfast haunted him for weeks. At night he would dream of her lunging at him with her fangs bared, and in the daytime he felt afraid that she would find him and eat him, or worse, eat one of the other birds. He began to lose interest in the fat juicy worms at the river bank, wondering if they felt the same about being eaten by him. Did they sleep at night, dreaming of big birds who would come and pull them from the safe, cool earth, and make them into breakfast?

The other birds had noticed the change in him, and saw that he looked nervous and worried, and particularly ruffled these days, and so they asked him what was troubling him. At first he told them that he was fine, and that nothing was troubling him, before he again returned to nervously looking over his shoulder, and looking distracted. Inside his stomach was churning with fear, but he didn't want to get into trouble, or cause problems with the other birds. The second time they asked him what troubled him, he told them he was fine again, but the rest of the flock were wise birds, and they had seen this look before.

One morning, they flew down to the banks of the river, and bathed in the cool waters there. The little white-sailed fishing boats tacked across the wide breadth of the river, causing the water to wave out behind them. By the time the little waves reached the shoreline, they were gentle little things that lapped at the shore with the most soothing of sounds. Lulled into a soothing calm, and refreshed by the cool water, this time when the older birds asked the little bird what troubled him so much, he opened up and started to tell them about his adventure in the desert and the cobra that tried to eat him.

Their eyes grew wide as he told them his story, but rather than be angry with him, as he had expected, one of the older birds started to groom the little bird's feathers, and spoke kind words to him. The wise old bird told the little bird that the cobra and her kind were well known to them, as one of their flock before him had already become her lunch.

"And this is why we roost amongst the gaps in the temple walls," said the wise old bird, "because the cobra and her brothers cannot slither up to where we roost and take us unawares. It is safe there, and we can sleep soundly in the shadows."

The little bird began to feel some of the fear leave him. It was as if he had finally exhaled without ever knowing he had been holding his breath.

"She is mean and nasty," he cried, "and I hope I never meet her again!"

"She is just a cobra," the wise bird told him, "She is neither bad nor evil, and it is just her way. Just as we fly amongst the white clouds and bathe in the cool waters and eat insects, she slides along the ground searching for little birds and small animals to eat. She probably couldn't believe her luck when she found you out there in the desert, all alone."

The little bird sighed, and his feathers drooped again.

"But I feel so foolish," said the little bird. "If only I had listened to you all, and not wanted to go and prove how brave and clever I was, I would have saved myself from all this fear."

"Just like the cobra, fear doesn't have to be a bad thing. Fear is there to keep you safe," said the wise bird. "Just a little of it will stop you from venturing out into the wilderness without any protection at all, but too much of it can also hinder you. Imagine what would have happened if you had been frozen by your fear, just as the serpent was lunging towards you."

The little bird looked wide eyed, as if he didn't want to picture the image of him sitting unable to move as the cobra slid towards him.

"In life we have to learn to master our fears, or our fears will master us," the wise bird continued. "Think back to how you have been in the last few days, since you had your adventure. What has it been like for you?"

"Horrible," shuddered the little bird. "I haven't been able to sleep, I have pictured the snake every time I close my eyes, I have been afraid she will creep up behind me and eat me, or worse, that I would lead her back here unknowingly and that she would eat one of you instead, and then I would feel terrible always, to think that I had caused someone else to be hurt."

"And what does that tell you about yourself?" asked the wise bird, "What have you learned about yourself?"

The little bird thought for a moment, as the older bird continued to groom his feathers. He felt calm in the presence of the old wise bird, as if she knew all there was to know about life and cobras, and he knew he would always ask her advice if he wanted to know something in future.

"I don't know as much as I thought I did," said the little bird. "And that if I want to know about something, maybe I should ask someone who knows, before rushing blindly off in search of an adventure."

"Very good, you see, although the adventure was frightening while it happened, and the last few weeks have felt uncomfortable, do you see you have learned something, not only about cobras and the desert and about wandering off on your own, but also you have learned a bit more about yourself".

"Ah!" said the little bird, as the truth of her words washed over him like the cool waters of the river. "How did you get to be so wise?" asked the little bird, seeing the wise old bird in a very different light from the way he had seen her before. He suddenly realised how clever she was.

"I am just a lot older than you, that is all," she said. "I have lived a long time, and had many, many adventures, just like your adventure in the desert," she said, with a twinkle of laughter in her eye. "But whenever we have troubles coming into our life, the most important thing is to see something positive in them, for even the hardest time will teach you something you never knew before. And if we can always find that one grain of truth amongst the seeds of trouble, then nothing will ever be wasted."

The little bird nodded gently, absorbed in his own thoughts that were springing from her words like the green shoots of a new plant.

"So, if you were to feel an uncontrollable wish to go and explore and see what was beyond the Western hills, what would you do now that you didn't do last time?" asked the wise old bird.

The little bird thought for a moment, and then said, "I would ask someone who might have been there what it was like to begin with. And then I would share with them the wish I had to see what was there. And if my curiosity wasn't satisfied with the tales of the other birds, I would ask for a few of the birds to come with me so I could go and see for myself, and that way we could make sure we were all safe. We could look out for each other."

"Very good," said the wise old bird, and she yawned. "I think it is time for us to go back to the temple to snooze, don't you? It is getting very hot here now."

The little bird flew with the rest of his flock back to the safety of their roosting space, and as he began to close his eyes with sleepiness, he kept thinking about all that he had learned that day, and felt lucky to have had the chance to learn things and come out unscathed on the other side. And for the first time in a long time, he slept soundly and was undisturbed by bad dreams. In fact, he slept so soundly that he did not even wake up when the cool of the evening came, but instead slept right through to the next morning, watched over by the wise old bird as he slept.

When he awoke the next morning, he felt very cheerful and happy, and looked forward to a hearty breakfast and a nice dip in the river, content in the routine of the flock for several weeks before he even thought about having any more adventures. And it was several days later that he realised with a jump that he hadn't dreamed of the cobra and her snapping jaws for a long time. The image of the cobra had disappeared, and simply become a memory.

"Intelligent people know others.

Enlightened people know themselves.

You can conquer others with power,

But it takes true strength to conquer yourself."

Chapter 33, of the Tao Te Ching, by Lao Tzu

The Pixie Who Wouldn't Stop Talking

There was once a little pixie called Sylvie, who lived in a small cave in a Cliffside overlooking the sea. When the weather was calm the sea lapped gently against the shore beneath her cave, and when the weather was stormy, the waves would smash against the shore and send spray flying high into the air and into her cave. For Sylvie, the sound of the sea was always present, sometimes in the background like a low constant heartbeat, and sometimes louder like the sound of clashing cymbals and a loud drum all competing for her attention.

Sylvie liked nothing more than to go hunting about in the rock pools and on the beach below to see what the sea had washed up this time. It was a peaceful life, and she was very content, except for one thing.

In the cave next door to Sylvie's lived another Pixie called Smith. Smith was a nice enough pixie, but he did have one big drawback that Sylvie didn't like, and that was that he could talk for the whole pixie kingdom, and frequently he would try to. All day long he would talk talk talk if he could, and he never even cared if he got a response, just so long as he could keep talking at someone.

Whatever Sylvie was doing, she could be guaranteed that Smith would have opinion about it,

"You don't want to do it like that, you want to do it like this..." he would frequently say, before launching into a very long and very dull explanation of what Sylvie should be doing.

Well, Sylvie was never a fan of 'should's, and if a sentence began with 'you should' she invariably ignored what came after, but Sylvie was a kind pixie, and she suspected that Smith was really quite lonely (probably because he had talked everyone else into a coma) so she fixed a smile to her face, closed her ears, and looked as if she was listening while really inside she was not. As Smith was not the most sensitive or clever of Pixies, he did not notice that Sylvie was really thinking about other things while he talked at her.

Once, when Smith had worked up a particularly fine head of steam, he even followed Sylvie from one end of the beach to the other with barely a pause for breath. In fact, Smith was such an incurable chatterbox; he even talked in his sleep. The awful thing was, that Smith was so intent on voicing his opinions as much as he really could, he would even talk knowledgeably about things that he knew nothing about. In fact, Sylvie suspected that he mostly talked about things he knew nothing about, because if she ever asked him a question about one of the things he had been telling her she should do, his answer was often a little vague, as if he didn't really know about the details (because he didn't).

One day, as Sylvie was making her way slowly up the beach in search of pretty shells, half listening to Smith as he tried in vain to tell her what she needed to know about beach combing, she came across something a little unusual on the beach. There amongst the sands, she came across a small glass bottle that had something hidden inside it. But as the glass was a little smeared and misty, she couldn't quite make out what it was.

"You know what you should do?" said Smith, launching into a fresh topic as he saw what Sylvie saw, "you should smash the bottle, and then you will be able to see what is inside it."

"But what if it is a spell or an enchantment that has been deliberately put into the bottle to control it?" asked Sylvie, feeling a little irritated at Smith's silly suggestion. "Then we would be releasing something that we wouldn't want to release."

"Hmm, well, umm, well" said Smith, never even wanting to leave a pause in a nice state of peace and quiet."In that case, I know what you should do; you should take it to the sorceress who lives on the other side of the woods on the other side of the headland. That way she can tell you what is in the bottle..."

"Actually, that is not a bad idea," said Sylvie, for once thinking Smith has spoken some sense.

"And another thing," said Smith, "I should come with you, because I was with you when you found it."

"Come on then," said Sylvie, "If we get going now, we should get there by teatime."

Smith, suddenly taken aback by Sylvie's acceptance, said,

"Right, ok. Well then. Let's go. If we follow that path along the top of the cliffs we should get there fairly easily."

"I think you will find it will be easier if we take the path through the woods," said Sylvie, "Since the sorceress lives on the other side of the woods."

And without waiting for any further discussion from Smith, as she knew they could be stuck on the beach for a very long time if she did, Sylvie set off in the direction of the woods, with Smith walking a few paces behind, still chattering non-stop.

The day was beautiful and sunny, and Sylvie was struck by how pretty the countryside was where they lived. The sunlight danced off the beautiful green leaves of all the trees, as they danced in the slight breeze that blew off the sea. The path through the woods was dappled with green, and the air was nice and warm, and heavy with the scent of the summer flowers that bloomed on the ground amongst the short grass that grew in patches between the trunks of the trees. Violets lay beneath her feet and released their delicate scent as she lightly walked over them, here and there honeysuckle climbed between the low-lying branches of the trees, giving the air a soothing embrace, that was in stark contrast to the incessant chatter coming from the pixie who was keeping up the rear, and having to break into a jog now and then to keep up with Sylvie.

"Smith!" said Sylvie, perhaps a little more sharply than she had intended. "Could we just not talk for a while, do you think? The woods are so pretty, and the birds are chirping so beautifully, and I think we should really listen to the songs they are working so hard to sing us. Would you mind?"

"Oh," said Smith, slightly confused by the idea of not talking. "Alright then."

But it wasn't long before he just couldn't help himself. At first it started with a loud sigh or two, and this was closely followed by a clearing of his throat. And then within five minutes, he was off again, telling Sylvie about all the different types of bird song he could identify (even though she knew he got at least three of them wrong.)

Before long they reached the house of the sorceress, at least Sylvie knew it must be the house of the sorceress as the smoke that came out of the chimney in short round puffs was a dark pink colour, and gusts of wind kept blowing the curtains out of the windows instead of in. As they walked up the garden path, a small black cat sat on the doorstep, washing its whiskers.

"Can I help you?" asked the black cat.

Now to you and I, a talking cat may seem like the strangest thing, but of course Sylvie was a pixie after all, and in our world people tell us that talking cats and pixies don't exist, but of course Sylvie and Smith were both there, so why shouldn't there be a talking cat washing its whiskers on the front door step?

"Greetings oh wise and beautiful cat of the shining midnight coat," said Sylvie (for she knew how a cat should be addressed properly).

The cat bowed its head lightly in acknowledgement, and then turned to Smith to receive his greeting. Sadly, Smith had obviously not read the rule book on how a cat should be addressed, and instead of greeting the cat with suitable respect and awe, he instead scratched his head in confusion, and said,

"Well, cat. Where is your mistress? Come on, quickly, we haven't got all day. We are very important you know, and we have walked a very long way."

The cat, (whose name was Morgana) stepped aside in astonishment at Smith's rudeness, and watched him as he marched up to the front door and knocked loudly. The door was opened by a little old lady, who was wearing a very ornate hat with a large collection of fruit on it, and a long flowing purple housecoat. At the bottom of this, a pair of sparkling red shoes poked out from underneath. Smith decided he must be face to face with the sorceress herself, so he immediately launched into a very long winded explanation as to who they were and where they had come from and why they had come.

Meanwhile, Sylvie watched Morgana the cat as she stretched and yawned, and muttered "Yeah, yeah," under her breath, just loud enough that Smith could hear it, if he chose to, but obviously he did not.

Sylvie looked on with great interest and with a suppressed giggle on her lips. She liked Morgana the cat, as she suspected the cat would not scruple to say any of the things that Sylvie had secretly thought for a long time now, but had not had the heart to say out loud.

"Well," said the little old lady, peering through her half-moon glasses at Smith. "Perhaps if this is going to require some explanation, you should both come in and have tea with Morgana and I."

They went inside the little cottage, where a little kitchen table was already laid out with the things for tea, for Sylvie and Smith had been expected (of course). Before they had even sat down, Smith grabbed the little bottle from Sylvie, and launched in to an explanation of what he thought it was, and what he thought they should do with it. The little old lady simply nodded along, and interjected the odd "Yes, dear. Milk?" as Smith continued to ramble without any sense of how rude he was being. After a minute or two, Morgana began to cough, loudly.

"Oh dear, poor cat," said Smith, "Have you got a hair ball?" and he proceeded to tickle Morgana under the chin, as he then turned back to doing his favourite thing, which was of course talking.

Morgana was quite incensed by Smith's over-familiarity with her. Hair ball? How dare he! She again started muttering under her breath again, loudly enough that there was no mistaking what she was saying.

"Rude pixies! Coming into my house and talking talking talking without stopping even to be polite and thank us for the tea! I will give you hair ball! Rude little pixie..."

Smith, who was well able to hear what Morgana was saying and could no longer bring himself to pretend he couldn't, felt it was his duty to say to the little old lady,

"Madam, your cat seems to be extremely rude!"

"My cat?" said the little old lady with surprise. "Oh no, Morgana is not my cat... I am simply her human. I look after her and tend her needs and get the ingredients ready for her spells."

"Her spells?" said Sylvie with astonishment.

"Why yes, dear," said the old lady. "Oh goodness, you didn't think I was the sorceress did you?" and she immediately started to cackle, very loudly.

Meanwhile, Morgana the cat continued to lick her paws and casually clean her ears.

"Oh dear," thought Sylvie, realising just how much Smith had offended the real sorceress, Morgana. "This is not going to end well..."

"You, Mr Pixie, are extremely impertinent!" hissed Morgana, narrowing her eyes at Smith, and for once, Smith actually appeared to be lost for words, as he simply opened and closed his mouth like a goldfish, as no sound came out. "Yes, that is a distinct improvement," said Morgana. "Perhaps you can try keeping quiet for a while and see how you like that!"

As she said that, Smith suddenly realised that not only could he not think of what to say (although in the past there was very little connection in Smith's mind between thinking and speaking) but no sound would come out of his mouth at all. He stood in the middle of the cottage turning as purple as the old lady's housecoat with indignation.

"What lovely peace and quiet!" said Morgana, looking at the old lady and Sylvie, and completely ignoring the angry pixie in the middle of her living room. "Now, shall we have some tea and cream cake?"

"That would be lovely, thank you," said Sylvie, enjoying the company more and more by the minute.

"And you, Mr Pixie," said Morgana. "I suggest you keep quiet until you have something interesting to say. For far too long now you have spouted forth a load of old rubbish, without knowing if what you said was true or not." She wagged a claw at him as she spoke. "Now you can just keep quiet until you know what you are talking about."

Smith, severely chastened by the angry cat, sat quietly at one end of the table, sipping his tea as the old lady, Morgana and Silvie chattered over tea about the mysterious bottle and what might be in it.

"Well," said Morgana, "I suspect it might be a spell that someone put in the bottle, or maybe a genie. What do you think, Mr Pixie? Oh, silly me! I forgot, you can't talk!" she made a sound that Sylvie thought must be a cat laugh, but it sounded a strange cross between a purr, a hiss and a cough.

"Perhaps if we wash the outside of the bottle we might be able to see in?" suggested Sylvie.

"Well, that is a good idea," said the old lady. "Morgana, shall we wipe it with some of that 'see clearly' potion you made last week?"

The cat nodded briefly, and the old lady got up and walked over to the sideboard, where a colourful array of bottles and jars stood, arranged carefully with their labels facing outwards. Sylvie noticed there was quite a range of potions. In one brief glance, she saw 'to stop nosiness' and 'to make cloudy skies blue' and a rather fetching pink coloured potion that was called 'to appear beautiful'.

"Of course I don't need the 'appear beautiful" potion," said Morgana, preening her whiskers with a smile. "I am purrrrfect as I am."

The old lady made her way back to the table, uncorking the 'see clearly' bottle as she walked. Unfortunately for both of them, just at the point she had uncorked the bottle, she tripped over one of Morgana's catnip toys and managed to drop the entire contents of the bottle down Smith's neck. He jumped up with an astonished look on his face.

"Oh dear," said Morgana. "He's just had a lifetime of ignoring other people's feelings go down the back of his neck with a splash. All those things he has been ignoring all that time have all just landed with a whoosh! Well, this ought to be interesting; perhaps I should let him talk for this part."

She waved her paw in Smith's direction, and he opened his mouth to speak.

"Oh my goodness!" he exclaimed. "Is that really what I have been like?" he looked at Sylvie, and she grimaced slightly at him, but then nodded her head. "Oh my goodness. I am so terribly sorry!" and with this, he sat down and took a large gulp of his tea.

Well, from that day on, Smith never did chatter on like he did before and instead he would only speak when he had something particularly important to say. But if anyone asked about the sorceress that lived across the headland, he would speak of Morgana in glowing terms as being the most beautiful and gracious and wise cat there ever was.

So now Sylvie was able to sit outside her cave and enjoy afternoon tea with Smith as they sat and listened to the waves beneath them, or just sat and enjoyed each other's company.

"And what about the bottle?" you might ask. "What was in the bottle?" Well, after they had enjoyed their tea and cake, Morgana took the old lady and both Pixies out into the garden to uncork the bottle, as she said it would be much safer to do if they were outside in the open air. And what do you think was in the bottle?

Just a lot of old salty sea water and some sand of course!

"Those who know do not speak,

Those who speak do not know."

"Heaven and Earth are like a set of bellows.

Although empty, they are endlessly productive.

The more you work, the more they produce.

The mouth on the other hand becomes exhausted if you talk too much.

Better to keep your thoughts inside you."

The Tao Te Ching by Lao Tzu

The Blacksmith of Postbridge

Once upon a time, a long time ago, there was a very talented blacksmith, who lived in a little village called Postbridge, which sat on top of a high moorland. In spring the primroses bloomed like a carpet of yellow beneath the tall beech trees. In summer the purple heather embraced the hillsides, in autumn the hedgerows were heavy with blackberries and in winter the wind rattled the slates on the roofs of the little houses and whipped across the faces of the local people, making them wrap themselves up in tight bundles of woollen scarves and hats.

The young blacksmith was the best blacksmith for miles around, and people in the neighbouring villages would talk to each other about how good his cooking pots were, how well he shod their horses, and how beautiful his cast iron work was. He worked so carefully and with such precision, that they secretly thought his fires must be tended by fairies and his hammer wielded under the protection and power of a force greater than him alone. The blacksmith knew the locals all told each other tales about his seemingly magical work, but he was a modest man, and rather than let his pride become swollen under the influence of such stories, it just spurred him on to learning more techniques, and becoming better at his craft.

The blacksmith had a sweetheart who lived in the village with her mother and father on their farm, and he knew that if he were to be able to ask her for her hand in marriage, as he hoped to, he would need to be able to show her that he could provide them with a good home. To do this, he wanted to absolutely know he was the best blacksmith in the county, to know in his heart as well as to hear it from the mouths of the villagers.

The blacksmith knew that Postbridge was a small village, and somehow he thought that he might be able to learn more and get more work if he just looked a little harder. So he decided to close up his forge for a few weeks, and travel to the nearest town, Tavistock, to look for it.

He got up very early one morning, loaded up his pony and began his journey, anticipating all the new things he would learn in Tavistock, and all the work he would get as a result. He trudged uphill and downhill, feeling the warm sunshine on his face and enjoying the walk immensely as he listened to the sound of the skylarks flying overhead, which told him that summer was truly here. The white fluffy clouds followed him across the sky and he whistled to himself as he walked.

After a time, the blacksmith began to feel a little tired, the hills seemed to get steeper, the sun disappeared behind the clouds and the skylarks themselves seemed to stop singing. He realised the pony was tired too as it was stumbling amongst the tuffets of grass, so the blacksmith stopped beside one of the many little brooks which criss-crossed the open moorland, and let his pony nibble on some nice grass, while he unpacked some bread and cheese that he had had the foresight to pack in his bag that morning. He could see Tavistock sitting deep in the valley ahead, and realised that it was a very long walk from Postbridge to Tavistock, but setting his mind on the thought of all that he might learn when he reached there, he mustered up some more strength and got ready to press on further.

He walked down the last hill, and as he did so, the countryside around him changed from the golden flowered gorse of the open moorland to the deep green fields and hedges, which bloomed with dog roses and wound their way downwards towards the town. The pony plodded on beside him, uncomplaining and swishing its tail to move the annoying flies which buzzed around its flanks.

By the time he reached Tavistock, it was late in the afternoon, so he made his way to an inn which was able to stable the pony overnight, and then decided to walk around the town to have a look round. He had been to Tavistock before for market days, but it was some years since he had been there last, and he was surprised at how busy the town was. People seemed to be all over the streets, standing in small groups, catching up and greeting friends, while children ran through the streets playing.

The blacksmith felt quite overwhelmed by the noise and the bustle at first, until he reminded himself that Postbridge was a quiet little village, and it was no wonder he was so taken aback at the sights and sounds of the market town. He wondered how he would ever be able to deal with a city like Plymouth or Exeter, and shuddering slightly at the thought, he walked on, trying to relax himself and just enjoy the atmosphere of the town.

After a while he realised he wasn't sure where the blacksmith's forge in Tavistock was, so he stopped and asked a man for directions.

"It be just over yonder near the river," the old man he had asked told him. "You be looking a bit worn out, boy. Have you come far?"

"The blacksmith smiled at the old man, and said, "Yes, I have walked from Postbridge today, so I am a bit worn out. But you should see the state of my pony..."

The old man laughed, and then looked confused.

"Well, I don't know why you came all this way in search of a blacksmith. There is a young man in Postbridge that does the finest work for miles around. I have heard tell that if he shoes your pony, the shoes will never wear out, no matter how many miles of road you take her walking along."

"Oh really?" said the young man, intrigued at this latest skill he had been given.

"Yes and his cooking pots make the finest stews from here to Launceston!" the old man said, and then waved a farewell as he went on his way, leaving the young blacksmith blushing slightly at the corner of the street. He only just remembered to shout a thank you to the old man's retreating back, waved, and then walked in the direction of the forge the old man had directed him to.

By the time he reached the forge, the Tavistock blacksmith had shut up shop, so the young blacksmith decided to go back to the inn and rest for the evening and have some food.When he reached the inn, he asked the innkeeper if he could please buy a meal.

"Take a seat in by the fire," said the innkeeper, "and I will send my Bessie in to see you. She will be pleased to sort you out with some dinner. Her cousin just came to visit, and she brought her a new cooking pot. She has been trying it out and will be pleased to have someone to taste the food."

The young blacksmith went and sat by the fire as instructed and sat back in a large wooden rocking chair that was facing the dancing flames. He felt soothed by the gentle rocking motion and the flickering orange of the fire, and he was soon dozing off in the chair.

A few moments later the door opened, and in came a rather round lady, who he decided must be Bessie.

"Evening, Sir," she said. "Frank said you would be wanting some dinner. Is that right?"

"Yes please," said the blacksmith. "What do you have?"

"Well, I have just been making a beef stew today. My cousin has just been to visit from Mortonhampstead on the other side of the moors, and she passed through Postbridge. While she was there she got me a new cooking pot from the blacksmith there. Well, I have never known anything quite like it!"

The young blacksmith felt a little overwhelmed by the barrage of words from Bessie, but smiled politely, until she mentioned the cooking pot, at which time he suddenly said,

"Really? What kind of cooking pot?"

"Oh, it is beautiful, Sir! It is a cast iron one, made by the blacksmith that has the forge at Greyhound in Postbridge. They do say he is a magician with his forge fire, and I have to say I never believed it before, but having tried the pot for myself, I am now inclined to believe them. They say he has the fairies tend his fire through the night, and that in the morning, sometimes the fairies have been hard at work with him and helped him to produce the most beautiful trellis work."

"Oh," said the Blacksmith. "Well, I will be very happy to try the stew for you and let you know how it is." He smiled to himself, and sat back in his chair, while Bessie bustled off into the kitchen, where he could hear a clattering of plates and pots, and then returned bearing a steaming bowl of beef stew and a large chunk of home-made bread, which she then placed on a small table which she pulled over to his chair. She then handed him a spoon, and stood next to him, adamant she would not leave him until he had tasted the stew and given her his verdict.

"Beautiful," he said, smiling at Bessie. She smiled, dropped a curtsy, and went back to the kitchen giggling with pride, and left him to enjoy his meal. As he took a second mouthful, he realised the stew really was beautiful, and he enjoyed every mouthful afterwards, until the bowl was quite empty. Then he rang the bell for Bessie to come and refill his bowl a second, and even a third time. Having stuffed himself full so thoroughly, he began to feel sleepy, and decided to go and check on the pony, before retiring to his bed, where he slept long and deeply until morning.

The next morning he awoke with the birds, and slowly remembered where he was and why he was here. The idea of learning new skills from the blacksmith here filled him with excitement, so he leapt out of bed, and dressed hurriedly. As he made his way down the stairs and towards the front door, he could hear the sound of voices coming from the parlour where he had sat last night. It was the sound of Bessie, talking loudly to some other women about how wonderful her new cooking pot was, and how the young man had not only asked for seconds the night before, but had then asked for a third portion as well. The young blacksmith smiled to himself, and then slipped out of the front door before any of the women could see him and embarrass him by asking him to uphold Bessie's story.

He left the inn behind him, and quickly made his way through the streets and towards the river where the forge lay. Already the streets were beginning to get busier, and he remembered that today was Friday which was market day in Tavistock. When he reached the forge, he stood some distance away, just watching people come and go. He realised he didn't really have a plan as such, he was hoping that he would be able to strike up a conversation with the blacksmith there, and ask him if he could stay and work with him for a day or two to learn any new skills he could teach him. The young blacksmith hoped that the offer of free work for the time he was there would be enough to persuade the Tavistock blacksmith that teaching him was a worthwhile task.

But for now, the young blacksmith was content to sit across the road from the forge, watching the work being done and seeing how the other man was working. After a while, his excitement seemed to get smaller and smaller, as he slowly began to realise that the Tavistock blacksmith's work was sloppy and he took a lot of shortcuts. The young blacksmith got a bit closer, so he could see what was being done, and he realised that the man's iron work was patchy, and it didn't look sturdy. He couldn't help but notice that when the man fitted horseshoes on a pony that had been brought to him, he worked quickly but not with the skill and attention to detail he himself used. He tried not to be critical, but watching this blacksmith working, he knew there was nothing for him to learn here.

The young blacksmith turned his back on the forge and made his way back to the Inn, his heart heavy with disappointment. He had walked so far and it was all for nothing.

Then he had an idea. There must be another blacksmith in the area. If he could find another one, perhaps they could teach him some new skills?

When he got back to the Inn, he found the Innkeeper and asked him where he could find a blacksmith, who wasn't the Tavistock one. The Innkeeper looked puzzled, and scratched his head thoughtfully.

"Well, now, let me think... The best blacksmith is found up in Postbridge, but if you don't want to travel that far, then Yelverton would be your best bet. That is about seven miles yonder," the Innkeeper said, gesturing in the direction he meant. The young Blacksmith thanked the Innkeeper, and then went to pack up his pony and set off for Yelverton.

This time the road was busy with other travellers, and the young blacksmith had the company of a tinker on the road for most of the way. They chatted together and passed the time of day, swapping tales and tips of where to stay. In fact, it was the tinker that did most of the talking while the blacksmith just listened, but he didn't mind, as it made the journey pass more quickly and the walk seem easier.

"What do you be travelling to Yelverton for then boy?" asked the Tinker at one point, for in this part of the country all the men were referred to as "boy" while all the women were referred to as "maid".

"I am going to seek the best blacksmith in the county," the young man said, "so he can teach me new things and I can find more work.

"Ah!" said the Tinker, "but in that case, you be travelling in the wrong direction," he said. "If it is the best blacksmith you want, then you will be wanting Postbridge, but it is way over them hills there, on the High Moor."

"Really?" said the young blacksmith, beginning to feel a sense of irritation.

"Ah," said the tinker knowingly. "I have heard all sorts of tales about the magic that goes on inside that smithy, I have heard he does magic with that forge fire. They say that if he shoes your pony for you, she will become as sure footed and delicate as an Arabian mare."

The two men walked on to Yelverton, and parted ways just outside the village, much to the relief of the young blacksmith. This quest was really frustrating him now; all he wanted to do was find someone to teach him how to be a better blacksmith, so he could feel confident and find more work, and be the best craftsman he could be. Why was it proving to be so difficult?

Once he reached Yelverton, it was easy to find the blacksmith's forge, as it was just behind a row of shops on the main street, and the young man could hear the familiar clang of hammer on metal, followed closely by the loud hissing as the blacksmith plunged his work into a barrel of cold water to cool it down. The young man walked up to the forge and nodded in greeting to the blacksmith.

"Alright young man?" the older blacksmith nodded, and went back to his task. The young blacksmith watched for a few minutes to see the quality of the man's work, and he was satisfied that this man's work was very good. He took a deep breath to steady his nerves, and then explained to the older blacksmith who he was and why he was there. The older blacksmith looked thoughtful as he listened to the young man, and gave him a fair hearing.

"And you say you are from Postbridge?" the older man asked. The young man nodded. ""And do you have some of your work with you?"

The younger man asked the older man to wait a moment while he walked over to the pony and reached into his saddlebags. He brought back some decorative items he had made, and handed them to the older blacksmith to have a look at. The older man turned them over in his hand, and looked up with a face full of admiration.

"I have seen your work before, but I could barely believe it," the older man said. "How do you get your scroll work to look so delicate and so even? I can see why folks think it is fairy-forged."

"Oh, I can show you if you like," the younger man said. The older man nodded, and so he and the younger man spent the rest of the day working in the forge while the young man showed the older man how he worked. In fact, they were so intent on what they were doing; they worked long into the night.

The next day, the young man said his goodbyes to the older blacksmith and promised he would return to show the older man some more of his secrets soon. Then he packed up his pony once more, and set out for home. As he walked up the steep hill towards the High Moor, he pondered the few days he had spent in the valley, and all the new things he had learned, going through it like a list in his head as he walked. After a few minutes, he began to realise that he had learned all sorts of truths about life and how to navigate his way through it, but he had learned no new forging techniques at all. In fact, he had taught someone else some of his own techniques, but not been given any new ones in return.

This was completely the opposite of what he had set out to do, which made him feel as if his journey had been a complete waste of time. He hadn't learned any new skills, so he wouldn't gain any more work as a result of his trip, so the whole thing had been pointless. His shoulders drooped, and his head dropped, and his footsteps felt heavy all the way home.

By the time the blacksmith reached his own forge in Postbridge, it was all he could do to take the packs off the pony and put the poor old girl into her stable before he went into his little house and fell onto his bed like a dead weight. He didn't even remove his muddy and travel worn boots; he just fell onto the bed and slid into a deep sleep, and slept long until the sun rose high in the sky over the river the next morning.

When he awoke the next morning, it took him a moment or two to remember he was back at home and in his own bed. His head felt heavy with sleep, and so he got out of bed and went outside to the yard to look at the morning and try and wake himself up. He thought maybe some cold water would wake him up and lift the fog from his brain, so he went over to the water pump, and started to pump the cold water with his right arm. As soon as he had a steady and strong flow of water going, he plunged his head into the full force of the water. The water, which came out of a spring beneath the ground, was crystal clear and icy cold. The cold of the water hit his head like his own hammer hitting the anvil, and as it did he let out an involuntary shout, as all the air was sucked out of his lungs. He ran a hand over his face and then came up for air, shaking his head like a wet dog.

As he looked up and wiped the water from his face with the front of his shirt, he suddenly realised he had an audience. A group of villagers had gathered in front of the forge, watching him in silence, looking hopeful.

"Morning!" the blacksmith shouted, raising a hand in greeting as a deep blush coloured his face, and hoping the villagers would not notice. Fancy being seen in this state by half the village!

"Morning boy!" old Farmer Mudge said, and it echoed around the group in a wave. The group came forward slightly. "You be back then? Back for good?" said Farmer Mudge, who had clearly been nominated to speak for the rest of the group.

The blacksmith nodded.

"We thought you might have left. Old Amyas came to get his horse shod two days ago, and he said you were gone and the forge fire was out. We thought you might not come back, seeing as you hadn't mentioned going anywhere to anyone."

"No, I am back. I just went to Tavistock, that's all."

"Ah," said Farmer Mudge. "And what were you in Tavistock for? The Market?"

The blacksmith realised that the group of villagers were intensely curious about what he had been doing, and they were not going to go away until they had got to the bottom of it. No matter how private he would like to have kept things, in the village most people knew what everyone else was doing, and if they didn't, they felt uncomfortable. He realised he may as well give in to it now and save them all a lot of time. He sighed.

"I went to Tavistock," he said, "to look for a skilled blacksmith."

"Really?" asked Mudge, with a laugh.

"Yes, really," said the blacksmith, a little irritated.

"A skilled blacksmith?" repeated Mudge, "what would you be wanting with one of those?"

The blacksmith couldn't help but notice that the group were looking at him as if he had lost his senses.

"To teach me," said the young blacksmith. "I wanted to learn new skills so that I could get better and find more work. So I went in search of the best blacksmith in the area."

"Ah," said Mudge, taking off his flat cap and scratching his head thoughtfully. "The best blacksmith in the area, eh? Did you find one?"

"No," said the young blacksmith. "I walked all the way to Tavistock, and then all the way to Yelverton and back and didn't find anything. I think I will just have to walk further next time. Maybe Plymouth or further."

"No, boy," said old Mudge. "You were just looking in the wrong place, that is all."

Somewhere in the crowd, one of the women giggled, and the sound was stifled as a wave of shushing noises came from the back.

"You should have said you wanted to meet the finest blacksmith in the area," said Mudge. "I know him well. In fact, I will go a step further and tell you I know the finest blacksmith in the whole county."

"Really?" said the young blacksmith, his eyes shining with excitement. "Where is he?" The young blacksmith finally thought he might learn the secret of what he had wanted so much for so long now.

"Are you blind, boy, or just stupid?" Mudge said with another laugh that sounded somewhat like a bark. The young blacksmith shook his head, confused by the turn of the conversation.

"I'll tell you where you will find the finest blacksmith in all the county. Follow me!" said Mudge, striding off towards the river.

The young blacksmith followed Mudge, wondering where they were going, and the crowd followed on behind him, chattering nervously. Mudge walked to the edge of the river, where the clear water gathered in a shallow pool by the river bank. He stood and waited for the blacksmith to catch up with him.

"Here boy, are you ready? Look there." Mudge pointed towards the pool with his hand. The blacksmith was confused, but walked over to stand next to Mudge, and peered down into the water. "I'll tell you where you will find the finest blacksmith in the county," said Mudge, laughing. "Right here. People talk for miles around about how good you are. We can all tell you tales of people we have met who have journeyed from miles away to come to you, people from as far as Exeter and beyond."

The truth started to dawn on the young man, and he realised how foolish he had been. The one thing he had been seeking all along was technical knowledge and skill from someone and his search had made him completely miss the fact that he already had it. He didn't need to find it somewhere outside, as he had it inside all along. If only he had known it before. If only he had not been so set on going to find it somewhere else, so uncompromising in his determination, he might have seen it.

The blacksmith felt humbled in the presence of their faith in him, and also mindful that he owed them a debt of loyalty and gratitude for their confidence in his abilities, and their willingness to step forward and show they cared for him.

He felt a warm glow in his heart, as he thought about preparing the forge fire and set about his daily work, which after several days' absence meant he had much to do.

"So the unwanting soul

Sees what is hidden,

And the ever-wanting soul

Sees only what it wants."

Chapter 1 of the Tao Te Ching, by Lao Tzu

Pixie and Jerome

"Jerome! Jerome? Where are you?" a familiar voice called through the darkness.

"Here! I am here! Coming!"

Jerome stepped out of the shadows of the gorse bush, and ran towards his mother. Like all foxes, Jerome had very good night vision, and could see in the dark very well. He and his mother often went out at night more than in the day, because his mother, Pixie, said that the world was a safer place in the dark. There was less chance of being chased by the hounds that hunted through the day, and less chance of being shot at by the farmer who was protecting his chickens as far as he was concerned.

"Why do they all want to kill us, Pixie?" Jerome frequently asked his mother.

"Because they think we are bad," said Pixie. "We eat their chickens sometimes, and they have the idea that the chickens belong to them, and that we are stealing."

"And are we stealing?" asked Jerome.

"That is a tricky question to answer," said Pixie. "Foxes do not own anything; we are just living our lives. We live, we eat, and we die, just as the chickens do. There is life and there is death, and in between there are many experiences. But I think the idea of owning another creature's life is a strange idea. Besides, if we didn't eat their chickens from time to time, we would go hungry, and they wouldn't scruple to eat the chickens themselves."

"And are we bad?" Jerome asked.

"No son, we are just foxes. We are neither good nor bad, like any other living thing, we just are."

Jerome found the idea of this quite puzzling. The world seemed to him to be full of contrasts and contradictions. There was good and bad, black and white, male and female, night and day, love and hate. After a few moments of contemplating this, he asked Pixie,

"Why are there so many opposites in life, Mum? Everything seems to be divided up into opposites... why?" for Jerome was a clever little fox cub who always liked to ask why.

Pixie thought carefully for a moment before asking.

"Jerome, the contradictions in life are really an illusion, they don't really exist. They only serve as a way for us to see meaning in the world around us, but they are just labels that make life seem more complicated than it really is.It is really a human invention that even we foxes have started to absorb. If you stop trying to become something and be content to just be, they you will do well in life and become a wise and cunning fox, like your father was." Here Pixie sighed, and looked sad.

"Tell me again the story of my Dad," said Jerome.

"But I tell you all the time," said Pixie, nudging Jerome affectionately with her nose.

"I know," said Jerome, "but it helps me to remember him. You know I was such a tiny little cub when we lost him."

"I know," said Pixie. "Where do you want me to start?"

"At the beginning," said Jerome.

"Well, your father and I met when we were both young foxes," said Pixie. "He had left his family earth in search of new territory, and somehow he stumbled into my territory. At first we didn't like each other at all. He wasn't what you would call a handsome fox as by then he was already battle scarred, but as I have told you before, handsome is just another contrast to ugly, and in life its meaning is only an illusion. Over time both things fade and all you are left with is what is on the inside. Of course now I know not to judge a character on the contrasts, but then I did not have the benefit of that knowledge. I thought he was an ugly fox, and I wanted him to go away and leave me alone.

Then one day, he caught a rabbit and left it outside my earth. I could smell the scent of the fresh meat, and I was very hungry. And when I came out to investigate, there he was, sitting quietly and patiently waiting for me, just a few feet away. We got to know each other over the next few weeks, and I grew to love him immensely. He was always very clever, and very funny. We would play together like cubs, and life was very happy.

The night we lost him, you were only a tiny little cub. It was only a few weeks after you were born, and it was a cold and blustery night. You and I were snuggled up in the earth, keeping warm together, and your father went out in search of food for us. When he hadn't come back by the next morning, I knew something had happened to him, so I went out looking for him, leaving you safely tucked up and sleeping.

I found what had happened, after an hour or two of following his trail. I followed his scent over to the farm over the hill there, and found a patch of grass that was marked by what had happened to him." Pixie sighed and went on. "Jerome, we need to start remembering something other than his death; your father loved us both very much, and was a happy fox. He lived his life to the full. He would not want us to remember how he died in battle with the hounds. We need to start rebuilding our happy memories, you know."

"You are right. Sometimes I get so angry Mum, as it feels so unfair. Why can't we all be together like before? Why can't we be a normal family?"

Pixie laughed and asked Jerome, "What is 'normal' Jerome? Normal doesn't exist. It is just another idea we use to compare things, but it is not really helpful. I have known many families, but they have all been different. I don't think I have ever met anyone who would say they were 'normal'. And as for feeling angry that life is unfair, just as we foxes are neither good nor bad, but just are, life is that way too. We tend to think of things as being good or bad, but really they are just experiences and they are neither. "

"What do you mean?" asked Jerome, not really following Pixie's train of thought.

"Well, my mother used to say, it is not the adder's bite that kills the unwary fox, it is the poison that kills. What she meant was it is not the experience that harms or helps us, but the meaning we give that experience. Two foxes may experience exactly the same event, but each one will give it a different meaning in their experience and their memories. The meaning we give it is what gives us the feeling we attach to it. Each fox's memories are unique to it, and this life is one of learning – each thing that happens teaches us something now, and when we have learned that lesson we move on to the next one. The contrasting feelings we give the events teach us that lesson. For instance, how could you know what sad was, if you had not felt what happy was? But an event that makes one fox sad, can be freeing for another; an event that can be happy for one, can be sad for another. "

Jerome sighed heavily and thought about this for a few moments.

"So how could I know peacefulness, if I didn't know what anxious felt like?"

"Exactly," said Pixie. "You know what things feel like inside of you. You know how comfortable it feels when you are curled up safely inside the earth with me, and you know how unpleasant it feels when we run away from the humans. Those feelings can help you in life."

"How?" asked Jerome.

"By telling you which way to go. If you are not sure which direction to go in, then see how it feels on the inside. If a certain way feels bad inside, then change it. All we have to navigate are our wits and our instincts and more importantly, our feelings which guide us into knowing what our instinct is trying to tell us. What better way to live?"

"But what about my father?" asked Jerome. "Why did he have to die? Was he not clever enough?"

"Ah, Jerome," said Pixie. "Your father was immensely clever and cunning. But sometimes bad things happen and you can't avoid them. It is like the great spirit has agreed with you that it is time to go, and we can't always argue with this. Your father's life ended, which was only natural for him, part of the endless cycle of life, and in order to know life, we must know death also. But for you and I, it will have taught us a different lesson. You and I know what it is to love someone and lose someone dear. You and I also know how precious we are to each other. You and I know how much we love and treasure each other. For that I am grateful, because some foxes never get to realise that until it is too late and it is gone. And you Jerome are my great treasure in life."

Jerome knew he was lucky to have a mother as wise as Pixie, and he checked inside and realised he did indeed feel warm and safe and loved. Yawning, he curled up into a little ball and tucked himself in next to Pixie, and fell fast asleep, and dreamt of running through the open fields, enjoying the sunshine, with his father and Pixie beside him.

"Things only seem beautiful to us because there are ugly things to compare them to.

In the same way, things only seem good to us because there are bad things.

This is why we can't have something without being able to lose it.

We can't do easy things without knowing what hard things are.

There can't be anything long unless there is something short to compare it to.

Without a front, it doesn't make sense to talk about a back.

Since everything that is different is also the same,

A wise person does things without making a big effort.

He creates things without trying too hard.

He gets things done but doesn't take credit for them.

The work is done then forgotten.

When a wise person does things this way, they last forever."

Verse 2, the Tao Te Ching by Lao Tzu

The Clever Princess

There was once a young Princess who lived in a castle in a far away land. When she was a little girl, she had diligently started to read all of the books in the castle library, one page at a time, a little each day.

Each day when she had finished her reading, she went out into the castle garden, and would ask the castle gardener to teach her about one single plant. Then she would take out her sketchbook and her paints and delicately paint each flower, meticulously.

When she had finished painting, she would go for a walk outside the castle walls and explore a small piece of the countryside around.

The Princess enjoyed her studying, and her painting, and her time in the fresh air. Little by little, the little Princess grew into a young woman who was very clever, full of knowledge, and who knew the whole of the kingdom, inside out and backwards.

Far away on the other side of the kingdom, there lived a wise Witch, who had heard about the clever Princess and was curious to know if she really was as accomplished as all the people said she was. So she travelled across the country on the back of her snowy white goat, (because the Witch did not like taking the train as it was far too busy and cramped, and she found people were on the whole a little bit smelly) and she wanted to see for herself if the Princess was really that clever.

When she arrived at the castle gate, she banged on the door with her long staff and asked to be admitted to see the Princess. The guard opened the small window in the gate, ready to refuse entry to whoever was knocking so loudly, but seeing who it was, he gulped and opened the main gate at once, afraid that if he didn't the Witch might turn him into a worm for a passing bird to gobble up for breakfast. The Witch was not really one of those Witches, (for there are some nice Witches in the world, despite what some stories might say) but grateful to be given entry to the castle, she decided not to correct him.

She led her snowy white goat in through the castle gates, and left him nibbling grass and flowers in the castle gardens, much to the horror of the castle gardener, who was appalled to see his prized nasturtiums disappearing into the mouth of the goat.The Witch walked up to the front door of the castle and rang the bell.

"Yes, can I help?" said the butler who came to answer the door, looking down his very long nose at the Witch, who suddenly realised she must be quite a sight, all travel-worn from riding the goat, with her striped stockings all wrinkled down round her ankles and her hair all full of leaves and twigs. But as she didn't really care what the butler thought, she replied,

“I am here to see the Princess, Westbourne, and I am in no mood to wait.”

The butler, whose name was indeed Westbourne, was shocked that the Witch knew his name, and realising she must be someone of importance, he let her in without any further hesitation, just in case she could read his mind, or knew by some witchcraft that he had been secretly eating the king’s favourite chocolates that morning.

The now rather nervous butler led the Witch into a parlour where she could sit and toast her toes in front of an open fire, and await the presence of the Princess. He then brought the Witch a tall glass of ginger beer (for everyone knows Witches love ginger beer) and then left her to wait in peace.

Before long, the Princess came down the stairs, her nose firmly buried in a copy of the complete works of William Shakespeare which she was reading for the twelfth time (which some people say is rather good).

“Hello,” said the Princess, closing her book. “You wanted to see me?”

“Yes,” said the Witch. “I have been told you are the cleverest young lady in all the land and I wanted to see if it was true.”

“And how will you know?” asked the Princess, quite curious to know how she would be measured.

“I thought I would ask you some clever questions, and see if you could get them right.”

“So what is in it for me?” asked the Princess, “and more importantly, what will you gain if I am really that clever?”

“In asking that particular question, you have passed the first test, for most people would not be clever enough to ask,” said the Witch. “If I am satisfied that you are indeed the cleverest girl in the entire kingdom, then I will grant you three wishes.”

“Aha!” said the Princess clearly impressed at the possibilities this might give her (because after all, she was a very clever Princess) “Please feel free to ask away.”

The Witch drummed her fingers on the end of her chin, pondering which question to ask first.

“How do you eat an elephant?” asked the Witch.

“That’s easy,” said the Princess. “You take one small bite at a time.” She answered; not paying much attention to the idea of what eating an elephant might taste like for she knew the Witch was asking her to explain her method of approaching the task and not what she thought the task would taste like.

"Hmm," said the Witch, this time placing her finger on her lips as she tried to think harder. "If I was to set off for Land's End now on a bicycle, and you were to set off at the same time on foot, which one of us would reach Land's End first?"

"That's easy, it would be me. If you were on a bicycle, you would have a long way to peddle. But if I was on foot, I could catch a bus to the train station, and then I would catch a train. Of course you wouldn't be allowed to take your bike on the train, so I would get there faster," said the Princess.

"Oh darn my socks with dental floss!" said the Witch, getting really annoyed as she didn't want to part with the three wishes too easily. "For your final question," said the Witch, pulling on the whiskers that grew on her chin as she thought even harder than before. "I have a riddle for you…

My brothers go round

While I am a star

Known for my beauty

I shine from afar."

"That is even easier than the last one!" exclaimed the Princess. "Duh! It is Venus of course. The planet has a pentagonal transit around the sun that takes eight years to complete, while the other planets have a circular orbit." She beamed at the Witch. "Satisfied now?"

"Ok, you win. I agree. You are the cleverest girl in all the land. Now I will be able to visit the Witches' convention next month and tell all the other Witches that my Princess is the cleverest of them all. They will be very envious. Right, I had best be getting back to my goat before he eats your whole garden…"

"Just a minute," said the Princess. "What about my three wishes? You did promise after all."

"Ah, yes," said the Witch, "but before you ask, you can't wish to have a thousand wishes granted, or a million instead of the three, as that would go against section three, paragraph four of the 'Witches' Guide to Wish Granting."

"And also section six, paragraph two," said the Princess. The Witch was terribly impressed, knowing that the Princess had read the almanac, but also slightly wary as she knew she had met her match.

"So what is your first wish?" asked the Witch.

"Well, firstly, I wish for all the people in the Kingdom to be healthy and happy,"

"How very wise of you," said the Witch, "granted."

"Secondly, I would like to know everything there is to know about everything, even things that are not yet unknown because we don't even know they are there."

"Are you sure?" asked the Witch. "Where would the fun be in that? Don't you enjoy the challenge of being able to explore things, piece by piece? The fun is in the journey after all and not just reaching the destination."

"Oh," said the Princess. "Come to think of it you are right. Let's scrap that idea. How about, 'I wish I could go on a long journey, travelling round the world and learning lots of new things about lots of new places'?"

"But what is stopping you from doing that already? You are clever, and you are a Princess after all."

"Yes, you are right again," said the Princess. "If I am so clever, how is it so hard to choose?"

"Because that is the nature of power, my dear," said the Witch. "Having the ability to do whatever you will, means you have to understand the responsibility for the consequences."

"Ok, I have it," said the Princess, struck suddenly with inspiration. "Do you know who the oldest person in the kingdom is?" she asked the Witch, and the Witch nodded. "I wish to give my second wish to them," she said. "I would like to give them their heart's desire."

"That is very generous of you, and does not break Section 23 paragraph six, contrary to popular belief, which states that in exceptional circumstances, wishes can be donated to a good cause," said the Witch. "Granted."

"And lastly," said the Princess, "For my third and final wish… I have really enjoyed our time today, in fact I haven't had this much fun since… well, ever!" she beamed at the Witch. "So for my third wish, I would like to be able to come and see you whenever I like. Can I?"

"Granted," said the Witch, "you may come and look for me, but there is one thing I must remind you of before I go. You have access to wealth and influence, and you have all that knowledge. Use it wisely" and with that she gathered herself up, and went to find her goat.

"A tree that it takes both arms to encircle grew from a tiny rootlet.

A many storied pagoda is built by placing one brick upon another brick.

A journey of three thousand miles is begun by a single step."

64th Verse of the Tao Te Ching, by Lao Tzu

Seth's Garden

There was once a young man called Seth, who wanted nothing more in life than to become a gardener. As a boy, his mother had given him a small patch of her garden to make his own and grow things in as he had said he wanted to learn how to tend plants. His mother had been surprised by his results, thinking that he might manage a small crop of geraniums or a few daffodils in the spring, but instead, Seth produced the most colourful corner of the garden that she, or anyone else in the village, had ever seen.

Seth's mother soon gave him the task of tending the rest of her garden, as it seemed that he had been born with the greenest of green fingers, and he even managed to grow plants that people said just couldn't be grown in that part of the country. Before long the garden was overflowing with beautiful flowers, and abundant vegetables and fruit.

Gradually, word spread about Seth's amazing garden, and people began to journey from neighbouring villages to see his prize roses and his rare orchids. After a time, word spread even further and people started to come from neighbouring towns to see the wonders that Seth could grow.

One day, Seth was busy tending his one true love, and whistling to himself happily as the wind sang in the leaves around him, when a man called over the little garden wall from the road.

"Afternoon young man, am I right in thinking this garden is all your own work?"

"Mine, and Nature's, Sir," said Seth. "I am just a servant to her, for without Nature's blessing, the plants would wither and die."

The man was impressed by Seth's humility, and saw potential in the young man. He decided then and there that he wanted Seth to come and work for him, so that he could teach him and also benefit from Seth's green fingers. You see, what Seth didn't realise was that the man he had been chatting to over the garden wall was in fact a very famous garden designer called Lancelot Brown, known in popular society as "Capability" Brown.

Capability Brown was the talk of his generation. Everyone of wealth or any standing wanted him to come and design their gardens for them. Capability Brown loved designing gardens with perfectly placed plants and trees, with perfectly measured form.

"Young man, if you come and work with me, I will teach you how to master nature so that you can improve on her designs and make your gardens even better," he said.

Seth wondered how this could be possible. He knew nature was the greatest designer there was, but he was willing to suspend his own beliefs because he knew that this way he might learn something new, and he knew that the greatest achievements in life were knowledge and understanding. So Seth agreed to Capability Brown's proposal, and arranged to come and work with him. So he packed up his belongings into a small bag, said farewell to his mother, and whistled to his dog.

Off they all set, down the long and winding road towards the large country estate where Capability Brown was working on his latest project, the complete re-design and remodelling of the vast grounds around a large country house. The precision with which everything was arranged quite took Seth's breath away. It conformed absolutely to the blueprint that Capability and drawn up and shown to him; the hedges were all clipped just so, the plants all grew perfectly neatly where Capability had planned or them to be, and not a blade of grass was out of place. The perfectly clipped lawns and carefully arranged hedges all served to emphasise the beauty of the great house all the more. A system of small ponds led the eye down towards a perfectly shaped and proportioned lake what lay at the bottom of the lawns, which then led on to the countryside beyond.

While Seth could see the beauty of the arrangement, and the skill with which Capability had designed the gardens, he couldn't help thinking there was more beauty to be seen in the wilder open country beyond, but knowing he was there to learn from a master, he put his personal ideas of taste to one side along with his feelings.

Seth decided to explore the gardens further on his own while Capability went to check on progress with his team of gardeners, who Seth would be working amongst the next day. Seth set off with his dog and walked along the gravel path that led down towards the lake. Although any one of the gardeners working there would have expected Seth to be bowled over by the perfection and precision with which Capability had designed the layout, Seth was remarkably unmoved by it. He sat down on a patch of perfectly cut grass with his beloved dog beside him, sighed and shook his head in wonder.

Passing gardener came around the corner of the hedge at that moment, and having heard that a new gardener was to come and join them tomorrow, he guessed who Seth was and came over to introduce himself.

"You'll be the new gardener then? My name is Samuel Green," he said, holding out a rather earthy hand to Seth.

"Seth," said Seth, jumping to his feet and grasping the other man's hand firmly in his own.

"So what do you think? Isn't it beautiful?" asked Samuel.

"It certainly is," said Seth, but his tone sounded a little unsure, and then he sighed.

"See how beautiful the patterns and forms are," said Samuel. "I think this garden is far superior to any other in England, if not further afield, and far superior to anything else in nature."

“I don’t know,” said Seth, voicing his dissent for the first time, for although Seth was a polite young man, he was also plain speaking when he felt he had the space to be. “Only nature can design a really good garden. Anything else is just temporary, and proof of man’s vanity.”

“What do you mean?” asked Samuel with a chuckle. “Are you calling Capability Brown vain?” Samuel had warmed to Seth immediately.

“No, but...” Seth faltered, not sure how to put his ideas into words. His dog sighed and lay down heavily with a grunt. “Where is the passion?” asked Seth. “Where is the feeling? Where is the colour?” Seth’s voice gathered feeling as he spoke.

“Who needs colour when you have such beauty in mathematical lines?” said Samuel. “Who needs passion when you can have order and form?”

Samuel couldn’t help thinking Seth was as barking as his dog, but as he was enjoying the debate, he decided to show Seth the rest of the gardens.

Over time, Seth and Samuel became very good friends; not the kind that agree on everything but the kind who enjoy talking and sharing their difference of opinions and ideas. They would debate long and hard over many topics of garden wisdom, and both enjoyed the spark they shared.

After several years of working at the same garden, Capability Brown, who was by this time an old man retired and went to live far away in the sunshine. Seth and Samuel both worked very hard, and Seth grew up to become the head gardener, with Samuel still working alongside him.

Over time nature started to creep back into the garden, bit by bit. The wind blew the seeds of wildflowers into the garden, so campions grew in the hedges and chamomile grew amongst the grass of the lawns, and Ivy crept in amongst the trees. The straight lines began to waiver, as nature had shown once more that this was her realm. All the people who visited the garden still thought it was beautiful, but now it was softer and less starkly contrasted with the countryside around it.

One day as they sat side by side surveying their garden and feeling a warm glow of satisfaction, Samuel remarked to Seth,

“Isn’t it a thing of beauty? I must say when you first arrived all those years ago I thought you were mad. But now I see what you mean. The softness of form is appealing, and I like the surprise that comes when wild plants creep in at the edges. Why only yesterday, I spotted a tiny fallow deer wandering in amongst the trees near the lake, and that would never have happened before.

Seth smiled to himself and patted his very old dog, who now slept soundly at his feet, soaking up the warmth of the late summer sun.

"A good traveller has no fixed plans and is not intent upon arriving. A good artist lets his intuition lead him wherever it wants. "

Verse 27 of the Tao Te Ching, by Lao Tzu

The Hairy Fairy

Once upon a time there was a little fairy called Isobel who lived in a large oak tree in the middle of a wood with her mother, her father and her sister Lille. Now, Lille was known for her sweet face and her charming personality. She was kind and gentle, and wise beyond her years, so the other fairies in the wood said. Isobel on the other hand was known for her fiery temperament and her tendency to lose her temper at the drop of a hat. When she lost her temper, all the other fairies would run for cover, covering their pointed ears as they ran.

If Isobel was out of sorts, there would be a great slamming of doors – BANG! And a great torrent of shouting – ARGH!

Isobel's parents despaired and didn't know what to do.

At the age of thirty when Isobel was still a little girl (for fairies live much longer than we humans) and her sister was just a little older, Isobel's grandfather came to visit. For some reason, that day Isobel was just very naughty. First she was mean to the pet butterfly who lived with them, by tugging hard on his antenna. Then she made her mother's best serving dish disappear in a puff of smoke. And then finally, as the family sat down together around the table to eat lunch, she threw a fairy cake at her father, and it hit him right on the head.

"That's it," said her father, who had tried to stay calm all day. "I have had enough of your bad behaviour young lady. Go to your room. Now!"

Isobel was in disgrace. She was put into her little bedroom to think about what she had done, but when the door shut behind her and she realised she was too little to reach the door handle to let herself out, she exploded in a fury of shouting and stamping.

Stamp stamp stamp! Argh!

Isobel yelled, and she screamed and she banged her way round her room, throwing things around and causing a stir, not only in her family but in all the other inhabitants of the oak tree as well. Outside the bedroom door, Isobel's mother stood with her grandfather, horrified at the maelstrom of shouting and banging erupting from the little room.

"Can't we let the poor little maid out?" asked her grandfather mournfully. "Let her out before she crashes through the floor and lands on the ground under the oak tree. You remember my great uncle Rumpestiltskin and what happened to him," he said, his voice dropping in volume as he mentioned what was the cause of much shame in the family.

"Oh, father," said Isobel's mum, "Remember great uncle Rumplestiltskin was very mean to the princess and he deserved what he got, but..." she faltered. "You are right, we should let her out."

Isobel was duly let out of her room on the understanding that she must behave herself and quell her temper, which she did... For the moment.

A few years later, when Isobel was forty, she had a terrible falling out with her sister. Lille had borrowed Isobel's favourite dress to wear it to a party, but had dropped a sticky piece of honey comb on the front of the dress, and had then tried to rub it off, which only made it spread further. Although it was not altogether Lille's fault (after all she was only sixty at the time) the dress was quite ruined.

When she found out, Isobel flew into a rage which lasted for days. As the rest of the family went to bed that night, and the next night, and the next night, her parents sat side by side in their bed, cringing and wondering when Isobel's fury would blow itself out. Eventually, after five days, Isobel lay in a heap in her room, exhausted, and slept, while all the inhabitants of the oak tree and the surrounding woods heaved a collective sigh of relief.

When Isobel was fifty five, and had been attending fairy school for some time, her parents had to go out for the day with Lille, and so they arranged for Isobel to spend that evening at her granddad's house. This put Isobel in a grumpy mood. It was not that she didn't want to see her granddad, for she loved him dearly and was always pleased to see him, it was just that the journey to her granddad's house, which was in a tall beech tree further into the woods took a whole hour, and she felt a bit left out of her parent's excursion.

"It is not fair!" she thought. "How come Lille gets to go with them and I have to go to stinky school?"

Granddad came to pick her up from school and was sorry to see that Isobel was wearing a very sulky expression. He gave her a hug and they set off towards the beech tree, along the path that led through the woods (for not all fairies fly all the time, you know, at least not where Isobel and her family came from.)

As they made their way through the wood, Granddad tried to ask Isobel about her day at school, but as she was tired and it was the end of a busy day, Isobel was grumpier than ever. After a time, Granddad decided to just let her be, and leave Isobel to her mood while he enjoyed their surroundings and the lovely walk home. The birds were singing in the trees, and squirrels ran to and fro, gathering nuts from the trees to bury in the ground and hide them away for when they would need food in the winter.

Just as they passed under a great hazel tree, one of the unfortunate squirrels lost his grip on a hazel nut and it fell down through the branches on its way to the ground, bump bump bump, right onto Isobel's head. Ouch!

"Grrrr!" started Isobel at once. "You stupid stupid squirrel! You should be more careful, you know!"

"Sorry! Sorry!" called the squirrel, making its way down through the tree, mortified and embarrassed that his hazel nut had hurt the unfortunate Isobel. "I am so sorry."

But however much the poor squirrel apologised, and however, much Granddad tried to calm her down, Isobel could not be placated. She picked up the hazelnut from the ground.

"Pigging thing!" she raged, "pigging thing hit me on the head!" and with this, she threw the hazelnut at the squirrel, aiming squarely at his head, but he ducked. The hazelnut flew through the air and hit a passing wizard, straight on the nose.

"Ouch!" he bellowed. "Who threw that hazelnut?!"

Well, Isobel had finally met her match in the temper stakes. The squirrel hid behind a tree in fear, peaking round it to see what would happen. But Isobel, who was still absorbed by her temper tantrum, continued to leap up and down, squealing about the hazelnut in her rage, quite oblivious to the angry wizard who was standing in front of her and looking sternly down his nose at her (the nose which was now glowing pink where the hazelnut had struck him).

Granddad started to apologise to the wizard on Isobel's behalf since she was clearly not going to.

"I must apologise for my granddaughter, Isobel. I am afraid she gets a little angry sometimes and doesn't realise what she is doing. I am sure she is very sorry – aren't you Isobel?" said Granddad, digging Isobel in the ribs with a finger. But this seemed only to enrage Isobel all the more, and rather than stop and apologise to the wizard, she just kept jumping up and down, howling with rage.

"Oh, Isobel is it? That Isobel?" the wizard said, even more unimpressed than before. "I have heard all about Isobel and her bad temper from my friend the owl who lives opposite the oak tree. He has told me he has been woken up in more than one occasion by Isobel having one of her tantrums."

"Oh dear," said Granddad. "I can only apologise again on her behalf."

"Yes, well," said the wizard, "Apologies are all very well, but perhaps Isobel needs to be taught a lesson or two." And with that, he took his wand out from his pocket, said some magical words, and a dart of white light shot out from the wand and hit Isobel right on the chin. "From now on, young lady, every time you lose your temper without a proper reason or a just cause, you will reap the rewards. In fact the rewards will start to grow on you immensely." With this, the wizard shook out his robes, and turned on his heel, disappearing into the wood.

Granddad looked over at Isobel, astonished. Whatever would her parents say when they got home? What on earth would he tell them?

"Come on Isobel, let's get home," said Granddad, but as he looked at Isobel, something very strange had happened to her. Her chin had started to sprout big black hairs, quite different from the blonde hair that grew on her head."Oh my goodness," he exclaimed. "What has happened to your chin?"

Isobel stopped for a moment, and took a small mirror out from her schoolbag and looked at herself.

"Argh!" she shouted, "What has the wizard done?" but as she became angry at the thought of the spell the wizard had cast on her, the hairs on her chin grew longer and she sprouted a moustache as well.

By the time Granddad managed to get her back to his house, Isobel had a very fetching curly black beard and moustache, well, it would have been very fetching had she been a boy. Isobel knew as clearly as Granddad did, that there was no point in trying to counteract a wizard's spell, as it would only make things worse. Isobel's anger started to cool as she instead began to cry.

"I have a beard!" she howled, "which is bigger than Professor Turvey's beard from school. All the other children will laugh at me and call me the Hairy Fairy!"

Granddad tried to comfort her, but she would not calm down. Later that evening, when she had cried herself to sleep, Granddad tucked her up in a blanket and tried to work out what to do. Should they try and find the wizard and ask him to release Isobel from his spell? All he could really do was wait until the next morning and see what Isobel's parents thought.

But the next morning, when Isobel woke up, her beard and moustache had disappeared. It was most peculiar. Granddad looked at her as she sleepily drank a glass of nectar for breakfast, and there was no trace of her former hairiness at all, not even any stubble. By the time Isobel was fully awake, she began to remember the wizard's spell, and again she started to feel angry. Within seconds her chin began to sprout hairs once more.

Granddad realised at once what was happening.

"Isobel," he said, "my dear little flower. Every time you get angry, the hair starts to grow. Instead of getting annoyed, try and think of something else. Quick! Remember how pink the wizard's nose went when you threw the hazelnut at him?"

Isobel thought about it, and smiled.

"That's it!" said Granddad. "Now, what else?" and then Granddad remembered Isobel was very ticklish, so he tickled her under the arm. Isobel howled with laughter and the hairs on her chin vanished.

For the next few days Isobel went through this process a few more time. Something would happen which would send her into a temper, but then just as her chin started to sprout its new beard, Isobel would then remember to change her thoughts and thereby change her mood. The most effective way of doing this she found, was to laugh at herself, which she found easy to do, because despite her bad temper, Isobel was not a bad fairy.

Over time it got easier and easier, and Isobel found that as giving in to her feelings and diving into them just made them bigger, by not allowing herself to really get angry like she used to, she felt angry less often.

Then one day, as she was playing in the woods with Lille, the wizard walked by once more. Recognising him, Isobel ran over to him. She noticed with surprise that she didn't feel angry to see him, in fact she felt pleased to see him, as life was much happier now she had realised she didn't have to be ruled by her feelings. They were just her feelings after all, and did not have to be all consuming if she did not chose to make them be.

"Excuse me, Sir," said Isobel shyly. "My name is Isobel, do you remember me?"

"No, I don't think we have met," said the wizard, "but I have heard all about you."

"Really?" said Isobel, feeling quite puzzled.

"Yes, in fact I have heard of both you and your sister Lille. It has been said that you both have the sweetest tempers and the kindest hearts this side of the great river."

"Really?" said Isobel, glowing with pride. "Gosh! Thank you."

"You are welcome, child," said the wizard with a chuckle and a glint in his eye.

"Nature rarely speaks

A whirlwind doesn't even last a whole morning

A rainstorm starts and ends in a single day

Such things are made by heaven and earth

If heaven and earth can't make a storm last

How can you?"

Verse 23 of the Tao Te Ching, by Lao Tzu

The Optimist's Journey

"Hey, Simon, over here!" the shout came.

Simon looked round, trying to work out who it was that had called out to him. The high street was busy with people browsing the stalls of the market, and Simon was busy unpacking the boxes of stock to put out on the market stall.

He had overslept this morning, just by a few minutes, but by the time he and Dad had got to the market, it was already filling up with early Saturday morning shoppers, who were anxious to catch the early worm bargains, before they were all gone. Simon had to work extra fast now to get the cards and gift wrapping paper that his dad sold out on display, but he didn't mind having to work extra hard now; it was worth it for the few extra minutes of sleep he had managed to steal.

"Hey, Simon!" the shout came again, and this time he located the sound. It was his friend Lenny from school, who was working today on a flower stall just two pitches down.

"Alright Lenny? How are you doing?" Simon said, slapping Lenny on the shoulder.

"Not bad, mate. Not bad," said Lenny, "although I could have done with not working on the stall today. I am knackered after going out last night!"

"Yeah, I know what you mean," said Simon. "But hey, at least it means we have some money for going out." Simon always liked to look on the brighter side of things, if he could.

"Yeah, I suppose you are right," said Lenny, "oh! And I saw you last night at the skate park with Jessica. Wow man! She is gorgeous! With a girl like that you need all the money you can get to keep taking her out."

"We're just friends," Simon couldn't help blushing just a little. "But yeah, you are right. She is lovely."

"Anyway, my old man will be back in a bit. I had better look lively. Are you coming out later?"

"Alright, see you in a bit."

Simon went back to his dad's stall, and kept working. His dad had just come back from parking the van, and had started to put the stock out as well.

"Was that Lenny Waite?" his dad asked.

"Yep. He's in my geography class at school," Simon said.

"I used to go to school with his father," Dad said. "Nice enough bloke, then and now, but the only thing I found was that he was a bit miserable," Dad said, starting to unpack one of the many boxes of cards, with a lightness of hand and a deftness that always amazed Simon. His dad was a big man, tall and very muscular, but surprisingly he was very sure footed, and not at all clumsy. He had been a rugby player when he was younger, and somehow he had never lost that level of fitness, and was very light on his feet.

"Miserable, how?" Simon asked, feeling a growing sense of familiarity.

"Well, I guess if you asked him if a glass was half empty or half full, he would always tell you it was empty. He was very clever at school, but if a teacher told him he had got eighty percent in an exam, rather than being chuffed about that, he would start berating himself for the twenty percent he didn't get."

"Ah," said Simon, knowingly.

"It was a shame really, because he was a very bright bloke, but somehow he kept missing all these amazing opportunities. It was as if he just couldn't see them."

"Like what?" asked Simon.

"All sorts of things," said Dad. "When he was fourteen the scouts from the football club spotted him playing with his mates in the park and offered him a place in their football academy."

"Really?" said Simon, clearly impressed with this.

"Yep! But he turned it down. Said that he thought it would be too much like hard work, training every day and spending all weekend practicing, and he thought it might interfere with his schoolwork. Just think, he might have been a Beckham by now but he never even tried. Now look at him!"

"Aha," said Simon, thinking that his dad's description sounded a bit like Lenny too, maybe it was a case of "like father like son"?

"He was clever though," Dad continued. "I seem to remember he got great grades at school and could easily have gone on to University, but he always said he wanted to start working as soon as he could, as he wanted to be earning money and didn't want to 'live on porridge for three years.' Just think what he could have been doing by now if he had gone," said Dad.

Simon pondered this all for a while, as he continued setting out the stall.

"What about you, Dad? Didn't you ever want to go to University?"

"Oh yes," said Dad. "I did go, for a little while. I did two terms, but then I lost my Dad, and my Mum asked me if I would take over the business for her, and I couldn't really do both things. Your Uncle Tom was too young to take it on, as he was still only fourteen then, so I felt I had to step in, as someone needed to support us all."

"Do you ever feel that you missed out?" Simon asked.

"No, not really. I prefer to think of it as just having had different possibilities, that's all. Soon after that I met your Mum, and instead of getting the possibility of the degree, the possibility of having you and your sister came about instead. I wouldn't change that for the world."

Simon suddenly realised that his dad tended to always look on the bright side of things too, so it was probably no accident that he did as well. He had always got on well with his dad, and always looked up to him. He was an admirable man in Simon's eyes, and any suggestion that he took after his dad made Simon's heart fill with pride.

That day at the market was a busy one, as Christmas was not far away and people were starting to think about doing their Christmas shopping. Simon found himself at the end of the day before he knew it, and he had enjoyed his day. He liked witnessing the interactions between people, and enjoyed being in the company of his dad too. The market was filled with people from every corner of the globe, all converging on this point now that they lived in this country. The food stalls consequently sold food from all over the world, and Simon enjoyed the sights and smells. But what he loved more than anything, was photographing the scenes. Each time he worked with his dad, he would bring along his camera, which had been a gift for his fifteenth birthday, and whenever he could get away from the stall for a break, he would get his camera out and start taking photographs, black and white mostly, as he liked the contrast and the way it seemed to capture a brief split second of existence for all eternity. The black and white prints seemed to be kinder to his subjects than colour, and also captured the intensity of their facial expressions in a way that colour film could not. When he wanted to capture more of the bustle and the high energy of so many people interacting together in one place, then he would switch to colour film.

Simon already had a reputation in his school as being a gifted photographer, and had already had one exhibition of his photos at an open evening at school. He hoped that if he could, he would go on to study photography at art school, but he had not yet broached the subject with his parents. He was not sure why, but he knew that he would need their financial support if he were to go to University, and this was so precious to him, that he was afraid of asking for help and being turned down by his dad.

It had worried him for several months now, and he wasn't quite sure how to bring the subject up with is dad. He was really waiting for the right opportunity to come, and he knew it had to come sooner or later. But what would he say?

Later that evening, he walked along the towpath that ran next to the canal that meandered its way through the area they lived in with Lenny Waite. They had finished up at the market and had decided to go for a walk and meet some of their friends from school. Simon was still mulling over the question of what he wanted to do with his life.

"Have you ever thought about what you want to do after school?" Simon asked Lenny.

"When we leave you mean?" Lenny asked, and Simon nodded. Lenny started chewing his lip slightly as he thought about it. "Well, I have had lots of ideas really, but no realistic ones. I don't think a single one of them would work."

"What like?" Simon asked.

"Well, to start with I thought about playing football, you know, professionally, but how many people actually make it? I mean, of all the people who go and slog their guts out through all that training, day after day, week after week. How many of them actually get to be selected?"

Lenny was so adamant, Simon knew there would be no point in challenging his ideas, so he just shrugged his shoulders, and Lenny continued.

"Then I thought about going to University and studying, but I am not really sure what I would study. I thought about English Literature, because that is what I like most at school, but I don't know where it would go. I can't see where it would lead to. Especially when you know what they say about arts degrees?" Simon shrugged again, and shook his head. "They are about as much use as a wet paper bag. It is not as if they lead directly into any kind of work, there is no logical progression."

"But what about doing what you want to do, just because you love it, and never mind what anyone else thinks or says?"

"That's all very well in la la land Simon, but remember we live in the real world. You have to take a balanced view of the options and be realistic about what is possible."

Simon thought Lenny sounded like he was using someone else's words. It was as if Lenny's dad was speaking through Lenny's mouth, and Simon could almost hear Lenny's dad's voice in place of his son's. It wasn't Lenny's language; it wasn't the words he would normally use. It wasn't Lenny's view of the world, but Simon suspected that Lenny got a steady stream of these ideas at home, and he had probably forgotten what his own views were by now.

They walked on, both deep in thought. Simon had thought about sharing his ideas for studying photography with Lenny, but after the conversation they had just had, he didn't want to share it anymore, in case it got trampled on and spoilt. He knew his dream was fragile, and he needed to shield it, to protect it from anyone who might not treat it with the delicacy of care that he himself gave it. He knew he had to shield his candle from the wind, in case it was blown out.

Several weeks passed before the topic came up again, but this time it was with Simon's dad, not his friends. They had gone out for day's fishing one Sunday, which was one of Simon's favourite things to do with his dad. There was something deeply soothing about watching the river just flow past them for several hours at a time, and it almost seemed immaterial as to whether or not they actually caught anything. It also gave them a long time to just catch up and talk together, some days about nothing in particular, and other days about things that were more substantial.

This time the topic of conversation turned to some real life-changing topics that Simon had been mulling over more recently. This day, the fishing seemed to be very slow, and Simon was beginning to think that he and his dad were just on a glorified picnic that just happened to involve two fishing lines, lined up on the riverbank and leading down to the water.

"I was talking to your Uncle Tom last night," said Dad.

"Aha," said Simon. "How is he?"

"He is fine. He was asking after you. He wanted to know if you have worked out what you want to do with your life."

"Oh, really? What did you tell him?" asked Simon. Curious to know how much his dad had picked up without them having actually talked about it.

"I told him he would probably need to ask you himself."

"Ah," said Simon.

"I always think there is time yet for you to decide. You have still got 'A' levels to get through before University comes into it."

"University?" said Simon. "So you think I can go then?"

"I don't think so," said Dad, "but I do hope so. I am aware there are certain things I didn't do and I would hate for you to not have the opportunities to explore life a little bit. Have you thought about it?"

Simon's stomach did a back flip as he took a deep breath and decided to jump in with both feet; it was now or never, he decided.

"Yes," he said, his voice trembling slightly and his heart pounding. "I was wondering about Art School," he glanced over at his dad to see if there was any sign of disapproval, but his dad's face looked remarkably neutral. "I was thinking specifically of photography," Simon said.

His dad nodded, and looked thoughtful, but didn't say anything, so Simon carried on.

"It's what I really want to do," he said, "but I know it is not very realistic."

"Realistic? In what way?"

"Well I know everyone says Arts degrees are pretty pointless, as they don't lead you anywhere," said Simon, thinking of his earlier conversation with Lenny.

"Everyone says?" said Dad, slightly incredulously. "Have you been talking to that Lenny Waite and his dad again?" Dad smiled, and Simon shrugged.

"I thought you might think I was being a bit flakey," said Simon. "I mean, I don't even know if it will lead me anywhere at this stage, but I can't think of anything else I would rather do."

"I am not surprised," said Dad. "I would have been more surprised if you had told me you wanted to study something like Business Studies, and I would have thought you were 'flakey' if you hadn't said photography. You go everywhere with that camera. Mum always says it is the best chunk of money we ever spent. I bet you even have it in your bag now, don't you, just in case you see something that you just have to take a photo of?"

Simon smiled and nodded.

"But what if I never find work at the end of it, what if I never manage to earn any money doing it? What if I spend three years studying and then find I have nothing to show for it at the end of it?"

"How could you have nothing to show for three years of studying?" asked Dad. "I suppose it depends on how you measure value, but I think that learning is never wasted, never. Even if you never get to practice what you have studied, the act of learning, of humbling yourself and acknowledging that there are things you don't know but want to know, helps you to grow as a person. So many people are afraid to admit what they don't know, so they go around in life with an attitude, trying to cover over their real selves, worried that someone will find out one day that they are just like everyone else; alone and afraid and vulnerable. And yet, what they don't realise is that it is our vulnerability as human beings that unites us, it is our very vulnerability that exposes our humanity and shows that we are all beautiful."

Simon learned a lot from his father that day, and it was one of those conversations that changed him profoundly as a person, and all through his life, he would find himself going back to that time, and leafing through the contents of his father's words, gleaning every last piece of wisdom he could find, even many years later when Simon was an old man and his dad had long since departed from this place.

"Hey, Simon, over here!" the shout came.

Simon looked round, trying to work out who it was that had called out to him. The high street was busy with people browsing through the shops, and Simon was busy unpacking a van which was loaded up with large framed prints, and carrying them into the gallery and studio he owned.

His dad called over to him to say, "That's the last one," and they carried it through the door of the studio.

"Hey, Simon!" the shout came again, and this time he located the sound.

"Hi Lenny, how are you? My god, how many years is it?"

"Too many to count," Lenny said, blushing a little. "How on earth are you?"

"Good, good. Busy but good." Simon said, as Lenny looked over his shoulder at the gallery behind.

"Is this yours?" Lenny asked, and Simon nodded. "I had heard you had done well for yourself, but this?"

Now it was Simon's turn to blush.

"Yes, it is mine. Some friends I know suggested I have an exhibition of some of my early work, you remember, the stuff I took when we worked down at the market, and it's the opening tonight."

"Wow, I remember. My god, we were both down there every Saturday complaining about not wanting to work and how boring it was."

Simon inwardly felt a slight jarring sensation; that was not how he remembered it. He remembered enjoying the market, and its energy, and it was Lenny who had done all the complaining.

"So what are you up to these days?" asked Simon, shielding his eyes from the sun with one had turned sideways on.

"Oh you know, same old same old..." said Lenny. "Dad is getting on a bit these days, so I am running the flower stall full time."

"Oh, ok," said Simon, surprised that Lenny had not moved on from there, but working hard to not let it show on his face. "Are you enjoying it?"

"It's ok, I guess. It is just as boring as it ever was, but it pays the bills I suppose," said Lenny, "I could never really work out what I wanted to do, so I suppose I just kind of stayed there, and it became a habit eventually."

Dad came out of the gallery, and spotting Lenny, came over to say hello.

"Hello Lenny, it's a long time since we have seen you. How is your dad?"

"Oh, he is ok thanks. He misses seeing you at the market these days. He always says he wishes he could retire like you did, but he always feels he has work to do."

Simon detected a little hint of resentment in the comment.

"Oh really?" said Dad, remaining neutral. "I suppose I am always busy too, but now I am helping Simon out, but yes, I do have time for my garden and going fishing when I want to, so I can't complain. It is a good life, that's for sure."

"Listen, why don't you stop by later?" Simon said. "There might be some faces you remember amongst the photos."

"Oh I don't know," said Lenny, his face looking more unhappy and frowning than Simon remembered him being before. "I think I still get quite enough of the market when I am down there every day." He shrugged his shoulders, then made his goodbyes and left.

Later that evening, in a packed gallery, a group of people stood around looking at one of the photographs in particular. It was a picture of two men, one older and one younger, and it was entitled "Like Father, Like Son – Possibilities".

"Interesting faces," said one man, who was standing on the right hand end of the little crowd, waving a glass in the direction of the print. "Somehow they both look disappointed, as if they never got their chances in life."

"Yes," said a woman in the middle, rubbing her chin thoughtfully. "It is almost as if the older man is a vision of what the younger one will become."

At that moment, Simon came over to talk to the group, as he was making his way round the whole gallery answering questions and making sure everyone had what they needed.

"Hey Simon," one of the men said. "What's the story behind this pair? They both look so miserable. As if someone really dealt them a bad hand in life."

"Oh, I don't know," said Simon, smiling. "They both had a good enough hand, but somehow they never quite saw it that way." He sighed, looked around the room with satisfaction, and caught his dad's eye across the crowded gallery.

Dad lifted his glass to Simon, and both men smiled at each other, both happy with their lot in life.

"Choose the positive – You have a choice – You are the master of your attitude. Choose the positive, the constructive. Optimism is a faith that leads to success"

Bruce Lee

Eko the Friendly Lion

There once was a friendly lion... for in some places in the world, friendly lions do exist you know. Lions generally do not like to talk about the friendly ones amongst their great Pride, in case word should ever get out and ruin the reputation they have worked so tirelessly to create. Anyway… there once was a friendly lion called Eko, who lived on the wide Savannah plains in the east of Africa. Eko lived with his mother, all of his aunts and step-mothers and his father, who was Head of the Pride.

Each day Eko would go out to the plains with his mother and the other lionesses, and watch from a safe distance as they went and caught dinner for the pride. He felt a little ill watching them, and always felt terribly sorry for the gazelle or the wildebeest that had the misfortune of looking like lunch to the lionesses.

"Sorry!" Eko would say quietly under his breath to the poor unfortunate lunch.

He wondered if any lions had ever been successful vegetarians, but the one time he had tried to eat grass it was very dry and tasteless, and it tickled his throat terribly when he tried to swallow it, and then when the dry season came, all of the grass dried up and disappeared. Eko suspected that unless he was able to grow a long neck like the giraffes, which was unlikely, he would be unable to last the summer if he were to try to be a vegetarian.

Once, he had even plucked up the courage to ask his father if he had ever met a vegetarian lion, as his father had travelled across the great plains and must have met lots of them, but his father laughed so hard that he fell on his back with his legs in the air, rolling in the earth as he roared with laughter.

Eko took that to mean that vegetarian lions were probably a rare occurrence in the Savannah, so instead Eko continued to apologise, very quietly, each time his family caught some lunch, and he hoped that wherever the spirit of the animal was, it didn't take it too personally.

Eko did worry what would happen if he were ever to be in a position where he needed to catch lunch for the rest of the Pride, so one day he decided to ask his mum about what he would need to do in order to not worry about hurting their lunch's feelings. His mother surprised him greatly with her response.

"Why Eko, you won't need to catch lunch," she said, looking sleepy in the sun after a particularly large meal, "You are the eldest male cub of your father's, which means you will lead the pride one day. You won't have to catch the lunch, as you will have lionesses to do that for you." And with this, her eyelids began to close, and she dozed off.

Eko however was now feeling very awake, and unable to doze now that his mother had told him that. Leader of the Pride? How on earth would anyone think he was strong enough or clever enough to be leader of the Pride? In fact, Eko was so shocked that he was unable to get to sleep at all for the next few days, so in the daytime when he should have been awake, his eyes were red and bloodshot, and his head hung low over his chest, as if it was too heavy for him to hold up.

He went back to his mother to ask her if she had been mistaken, just to be sure.

"Why no, Eko, all of your half siblings are girls. You don't expect them to lead the pride do you? Our pride has been led by your father, and before him your grandfather, just as it will be led by you one day, and then when you are an old lion, your son will lead the pride after you."

"Oh," said Eko, taken aback by all this new information and thinking it was a bit unfair that he got to lead the pride just because he was a boy. "But how do we know I will be clever, or strong or brave enough to lead the pride?"

"You will see," said his mother. "Just watch your father, and learn all you can and you will be all of those things. Your father is the best leader of any pride across the whole Savannah, after all," she said, with a hint of pride in her voice.

"But what if I am not strong enough? My cousin Effie is much stronger than me, she always beats me at play-fighting games," said Eko.

"But Eko," said his mum, "Effie is older than you, and that is why she is stronger. Wait until you grow up, when you grow your mane, then you will see."

Eko was very doubtful that his mother spoke the truth, and went away puzzled, to find the other lion cubs for a game of hunt and pounce. The other cubs were playing in the shade of a banyan tree, so Eko decided to sneak up on them and pounce.

"Roar, Rawr!" he shouted at the top of his lungs as he jumped out from behind a bush, but the other cubs didn't seem at all surprised by his "surprise" attack.

"We all heard you coming a mile away," said Effie. "Your great big paws make such a loud noise when you walk through the bush. You'll never make a good hunter-by-stealth. It's just as well you won't be a lioness when you grow up or we'd all starve!"

The other cubs giggled, and Eko felt ashamed and disappointed in himself.

"So how will I ever catch anything?"

"Through your strength silly," said Effie. "Look at your dad. When he pounces on anything he is strong enough to knock all the air out of it."

Eko tried to think about the times he had seen his father hunting. It wasn't very often and it tended to be more for entertainment than dinner, as the lionesses hunted very well. Occasionally when he was bored, Eko's father would yawn, stretch out his muscular limbs and then go off in search of sport. Eko didn't think he would like to hunt for entertainment, he would rather sit with the other lions and listen to stories, or make music, but despite the fact that he thought he might like to sing, he didn't remember the lions ever singing together. He had once watched a man-thing walking through the Savannah wearing bright colours and carrying a long staff. He had been singing at the top of his lungs as he walked and although he had been some way off, the sound had reached Eko, and he thought it was beautiful. He felt the song deep in the furthest parts of his stomach, and he wanted to follow the man so he could continue to hear the song, but his aunt had called sharply after him to call him back, and the sound had slowly faded into the distance.

Eko wondered if he could learn to sing. Perhaps if he got really good at singing, no one would notice he couldn't catch lunch. He thought about asking his mother about singing, so he went in search of her. She was sitting watching the cubs from a distance, so he walked up and curled around her legs, purring.

"What is it Eko?" she asked.

"Mummy, why don't lions sing?"

"Is that a joke, Eko? I am afraid I don't know the answer, but I am sure it will be very funny."

"No, Mum, it is not a joke," said Eko, feeling a bit downhearted. "It was a question. Why don't lions sing?"

"For the same reason that lions don't dance, Eko, it is not in our nature."

"Dancing?" thought Eko, "Now that sounds interesting!" (But he didn't dare ask his mother what dancing was all about.)

Eko went and sat by himself under a bush, out of the glare of the hot afternoon sun, and thought about giving the singing a try. He could just about remember how the man-thing's melody had gone. Eko took a deep breath, opened his mouth, and started to sing at the top of his lungs. The sound startled all of the animals and birds around him. The birds suddenly flew out of the trees with a great flapping of wings and squawking, and the lion cubs all stopped playing and stared in amazement. The gazelles on the plain stopped grazing and a far off herd of giraffes turned in unison to see where the sound came from.

Eko felt a warm feeling starting to swell and grow in his heart. So, undeterred by the sudden attention and unsure as to what the other creatures thought of him, Eko continued with his song. When Eko felt he had sung for as long as he wanted, he got up and walked to a more shady spot and lay down, feeling very satisfied with himself.

Effie came over and sat next to him.

"What was that?" she said. "I thought at first that you had hurt yourself."

"No," said Eko defiantly. "I was singing."

"Singing? What's that?"

"Something I heard a man-thing doing once."

"Oh," said Effie. "And because a man-thing does it, you think a lion can?"

"Why not?" said Eko. "We are the top of the food chain after all, why can't I sing if I want to?"

Effie didn't really know what to say then, so she didn't say anything else.

"Eko, your father wants you," called out one of the Aunts.

Eko suspected he may be about to get a big telling off, and his heart shrank a little. He got up and went in search of his father, who was lying on his back in the sun, soaking up the warmth.

"Daddy?" said Eko. "You wanted to see me?"

"Yes, boy. Come down to the water hole with me so we can drink," and with that his father got up and started slowly walking in the direction of the water hole. Eko ran along beside him, weaving in and out of his father's great strong legs.

As they approached the water hole, the background noise of bird-chatter suddenly stopped, which was generally what happened when Eko's father arrived anywhere. No one wanted to get snapped up in his strong jaws as an appetiser, so they fell silent and tried to be as invisible as possible.

"How are you son?" asked his father in between great mouthfuls of the clear, cool water.

"I'm ok," said Eko. "Are you going to tell me off for singing?"

"Is that what it was?" said his father with a laugh. "I thought you were practicing a new hunting technique with Effie, where you startle the lunch and then she catches it."

"No," said Eko, "I just wanted to try it, that is all."

“Well, I commend you on your creativity, son. No lion has ever sung before. What made you want to do it?”

“I heard a man-thing singing one day and I thought it sounded really beautiful, and he looked so happy when he was doing it, so I thought I would try it.”

“Ah,” said his father, “but why did you want to sing? I don’t mean just because of the man-thing, but for what purpose?”

Eko thought about the question for a moment or two before answering.

“Mother told me that one day I will be like you, and I will have to lead the Pride. And I was frightened, because I am not big and strong and clever like you. I can’t be like the lionesses as I don’t like the idea of catching lunch and even if I did like it, I wouldn’t know how. I have great big feet that mean everyone can hear me coming a mile away so I can’t be quiet when I am hunting, but I don’t know how to change it. I don’t know how to be like you. “

Of course you don’t Eko,” said his father. “How could you when I have never taught you?”

Eko’s face became a picture of astonishment.

“But I thought there was something wrong with me, so maybe if I got good at singing, I could do that instead.”

“A singing lion?” chuckled his father. “No, Eko, there is nothing wrong with you. I was just waiting for you to be big enough for me to start your lessons. You are an empty vessel waiting to be filled, and I didn’t want to fill you up with the wrong things. Maybe this is a sign that you are ready to start learning now. Would you like that?”

“Yes please!” said Eko, beaming from cheek to cheek.

So Eko started his lessons with his father, and learned many things. In time, he grew up to be a big, strong lion with the bushiest mane and the longest tail, and the biggest feet you could ever imagine seeing on a lion. But Eko never did give up his singing. It gave him so much joy. He would often stand on the Savannah, some distance away from his lionesses, take a deep breath and then sing with all his heart.

Of course, any passing man-thing may not have realised what Eko was doing, as they simply wondered why this particular lion was roaring so ferociously on the plains, but then, what would they know?

Thirty spokes unite at the single hub;
It is the empty space which makes the wheel useful.
Mold clay to form a bowl;
It is the empty space which makes the bowl useful.
Cut out windows and doors;
It is the empty space which makes the room useful."

11th Verse of the Tao Te Ching, by Lao Tzu

"We are what we think.
All that we are arises with our thoughts.
With our thoughts we make the world."

Siddhartha Gautama, Buddha

The Softness of Water

There were once two brothers who lived with their mother in a small house on the outskirts of a village. Their father had died many years before leaving their mother to bring them up alone. She found work where she could, but still the family was very poor, and they struggled to find money for school books and new clothes. She was a very proud woman, and she was determined that her boys would have the very best start in life that she could give them, even if that meant their clothes were patched in places, or that she would have to go without the little luxuries in life. Their mother worked as a seamstress, and she would work long into the night making fine clothes for the wealthy people in the nearby towns.

Of the two brothers, Frank was the eldest and little Peter was the younger by two years. Frank was six years old when their father died, and he remembered his father well, while Peter, having only been four when he died, had very little memory of him.Frank missed his father terribly, and always felt angry that his father had left them so early in life, and he felt a strong sense of needing to be the "man" in the family. He felt he needed to keep a strong hand on his younger brother, as someone needed to steer their family, and while he unconsciously resented this, those feelings just made him all the more determined.

Peter, by contrast, was a more gentle soul, and was inclined to be more easily swayed. Peter was a dreamer, and loved nothing more than to bury himself in a good book, while Frank enjoyed the rough and tumble of playing and fighting with the other boys in the village. Frank led a group of boys, who all looked up to him as their unofficial leader; he would direct them in the way he wanted them to go, while Peter preferred to keep his own company and his own counsel. He knew that in order to have a quieter life, it was better to go along with Frank's instructions. This would at least leave him able to slip away quietly when Frank's attention was diverted elsewhere, and go and sit in his favourite quiet spot, underneath the willow tree, beside the stream. The stream ran through the heath land that lay behind their house. When he sat down on the mossy grass he could allow his thoughts to wander and dream of faraway places and of wonders he had never seen, but wanted to see one day.

When Frank was thirteen years old, and Peter was eleven, their mother asked them to travel to a town that was several miles away in order to deliver a gown she had been making to a lady who lived there. She packed the boys off early in the morning with the carefully wrapped gown, a bag with some cheese and bread, and clear instructions that they should stick to the main road, and not accept a lift from any strange passing carts.

Frank and Peter set off on their journey just as the sun was rising up, turning the sky a clear shade of blue. There was not a cloud to be seen, and the day promised to be a hot one, so Frank was eager to cover some distance before it got too hot.

“Come on Peter, keep up!” Frank growled, marching up the road at quite a pace.

They travelled on for several miles before stopping for breakfast, both tired and hot, beside a bridge which crossed the same river that ran behind their house and seemed to be following the road. As they ate, they talked about the journey they had ahead of them.

“If we keep moving quickly, we should get there by eleven o’clock,” said Frank. “Then we must drop off the gown, collect the money for Mum, and head straight back home, if we are to get there at a reasonable time.”

“Can’t we just have a look around the town for a bit before we come home?” said Peter. “We will have walked so far to get there; it will be a shame not to see anything.”

“No,” said Frank, firmly. “We have no time for drifting about today. We have a very tight schedule to keep.”

Peter felt dismayed that he would not get to look around at the town, and would have instead to be keeping up with Frank’s strict pace all day, but knowing that it was useless to argue with his brother, because that tended to make him all the more stubborn, he held his tongue and decided to just wait and see what happened.

They soon moved on, under the sun which was now becoming searingly hot overhead, and reached the town a few hours later. The only problem was, Frank did not really know where the lady lived, having never been to the town alone before. He took them round in several circles looking for her house, convinced he could find it himself. Frank always believed that if a person was determined enough, they could do anything they wanted to. As they walked up and down the streets looking for the lady’s house, Frank became more and more frustrated, and having doubled back on themselves several times. Peter was enjoying the experience of seeing somewhere he had never been before. He realised Frank’s temper would only last so long before he really lost it and started shouting, so he decided to make the best of it while he could. Peter stopped a passerby while Frank was busy being annoyed, and asked for directions.

“It’s just two streets away in that direction,” the man said, waving with his arm to indicate where he meant.

“Thank you,” Peter smiled and ran to catch up with Frank, who was now a little way up the road, grinding his teeth with frustration, and getting more and more angry. Peter pulled on Frank’s sleeve gently, and said, “Come on, it’s over there.”

“Over where? Don’t be stupid Peter, how could you know where it is?” Frank replied, convinced (as always) that he was right.

Rather than argue, which Peter knew was pointless, he walked very slowly away from Frank, and started off in the direction they needed to go. He looked behind to make sure Frank would follow, beckoned to him and kept walking. Frank had no choice but to follow Peter, worried that if he didn't they would lose each other in the crowds, but all the while muttering under his breath with irritation.

Peter flowed in and out of the crowds of people, carefully and in his own time, and within a few minutes they had reached their destination.

Frank, who was feeling slightly embarrassed about being proven wrong, rang the doorbell whilst scowling at Peter. The door was answered by the lady's maid, who led the boys through a grand hallway which was lined with portraits of very stern looking people in fine clothes. They passed a dining room that shone with brilliant silverware and glass, and on down to the kitchen to wait, while she took the package to give to her mistress. Down in the kitchen, the cook gave the boys a cool glass of lemonade and some sticky spiced fruit cake, which tasted divine, and chattered merrily to them while they waited. The maid returned several minutes later with a smile and an envelope of money for their mother.

"The mistress is so happy with the gown," she said. "The mistress says there is no better seamstress in the county than your mother."

The boys murmured their thanks, slightly bashful at so much attention, and made their excuses to leave the house. When they got outside, Frank was fit to bursting about all the fine things they had seen inside the house.

"Did you see those fine paintings in the hallway?" he gushed. "They looked amazing, and all that fine china and silver! And did you see the size of that stove in the kitchen? So much bigger than ours! And fancy having a maid and a cook," he said. "When I grow up I shall have a house just like it. I won't stay in the village and be poor all my life, I want to be rich and live in a house just like that one, with a maid, and a cook and a butler! You just wait and see..."

Peter said very little, wondering only if their mother would want to live in a fine house like that one. Theirs was a simple life, but it was their own and at least they were free, in so far as anyone was. Peter had also noticed that the fine house had bars on the windows downstairs, presumably to keep unwanted people out, but somehow the house reminded him of a very fine cage.

The boys began to make their way home, leaving the town with all its bustling streets behind them. They headed out on the road that would eventually lead down towards their village, and prepared for the long walk home. After half an hour of walking, they reached the brow of the hill and were able to look down on the valley where the open road led down across the heath land towards the area where their village lay.

"I am tired of all this walking," said Frank, pointing to where the road wound around the outskirts of a forest and disappeared behind it. "Look there, I reckon we could cut through the forest and it would knock a good hour off our journey."

Peter shrugged, as he was used to Frank trying to push things the way he wanted them to go. He knew it was useless to disagree, as Frank would only win the argument anyway, even if it were by force, he chose not to remind Frank about what they had promised their mother that morning about sticking to the main road. Inside he had an uneasy feeling about this shortcut, but he consoled himself by focussing on the fact that it was a beautiful day, the sun was still shining brilliantly, and reflecting off the waters of the river that ran beside the road that led back towards their home.

When they reached the outskirts of the forest, they peered in to see what they could see by way of a path that might lead through the trees. The trees were packed very densely together, and there was no sign of any movement anywhere. The air seemed very still between the tall tree trunks, but they could hear the faint sound of the breeze blowing through the upper branches of the great tall pine trees, that sounded somehow like the waves on the sea shore, that they had been to see once with their mother. There was very little bird song, but the forest seemed peaceful to Peter, and the air inside was cool as the great branches overhead shielded them from the strength of the early afternoon sun. They walked a little way in, and found a path that seemed to lead in the right direction, but this was a slight miscalculation on Frank's part, because forest paths can often appear to run in straight lines, when really they curve around on themselves, and when all the pine trees in a forest can look very alike, it can be hard to remember which direction you should be walking in.

After walking for half an hour, Peter began to feel a slight sense of déjà vu. He was sure they had been past that tree on the right before, the one with the great crack in the bark where the aromatic pine resin dripped down the side of the tree like a rivulet of golden blood. He looked over at Frank, not sure if he should say something, and Frank seemed to be getting a bit agitated too.

"I think we have already been this way before," Frank said. "Maybe we should take that path up ahead that leads off to the left. Come on, keep up, I don't want to lose you in here."

They did indeed take the path that led to the left, but after another length of time, they again came to the same tree, with the same scar of colophony on its trunk. Frank swore loudly, and stamped his foot.

"I knew it," he fumed, "these trees all look alike. How can we find our way out when all the paths look the same?"

The boys looked in every direction, but all they could see were more of the same tall straight pine trees. They could not see a way out of the forest at all, and they were lost amidst the mysterious looking trees. Peter sat down on a fallen tree trunk, and opened his awareness to the forest around him, while Frank paced up and down getting more and more irritated.

"This doesn't make any sense!" he fumed, "This should be so easy. All we had to do was keep in a straight line through the trees, and it should have led us out the other side to join the road again. I don't understand it!"

Peter sat peacefully on his tree trunk, looking up at the beautiful green of the trees outlined against the glimpses of clear blue sky up above. He heard the wind as it sang in the branches, and stretched his awareness out even further to the deepest depths of the forest. Suddenly he heard a faint sound that was so familiar to him he had almost failed to notice it before. It was the sound of running water. He located the direction the sound was coming from, and got to his feet and started to pick his way through the trees towards it. Frank, baffled once again by Peter's behaviour, became irritated with his little brother.

"Idiot!" he shouted. "Where are you off to now? Come back!"

But Peter was lost in his own thoughts, and kept on walking, leaving Frank once again to follow on behind, muttering curses under his breath. Before long, they reached a clearing between the trees, and there, as he had thought it would be, was the little gurgling river that had followed them along the road, and would ultimately lead them back down the valley and into their own village. When Frank at last caught up with him, Peter was crouched by the side of the river, dipping his hand into the cool, clear soft water.

"Look," said Peter, looking over his shoulder at Frank, "this is our river. If we follow it, it will lead us back home."

He got up, splashing the water on his neck to cool himself down, and continued to walk steadily along the banks of the little river, which lead over rocks and through little pools, and down to the edge of the forest, where they found the road they had lost so long ago.

Frank was again frustrated to have been proven wrong, and he felt that Peter was trying to get the better of him. Peter's silence only seemed to frustrate him even more, and so they walked on in silence, with Frank marching ahead, and Peter trying to keep up with him. When they reached the house, tired and worn out, Frank threw the envelope containing the money on the kitchen table and marched off to the bedroom, where he slammed the door.

Their mother, taken by surprise at this rather abrupt entrance looked over at Peter with a frown.

"What is wrong with him?" she asked. "Didn't the lady like the gown?"

"Oh no, she loved it," said Peter. "She said that you are the best seamstress for miles around."

"So what got Frank so riled up? Did you argue?"

“No, not exactly,” said Peter, and started to tell his mother about all the wonderful adventures they had had that day. Of all the people they had seen, the shops and the carriages, the great houses, and the lady’s house with the big kitchen and the sticky fruit cake, and about how kind people had been to them, and about how they had lost their way, and how he had managed to find it again.

“Do you think he will be angry with me for long?” Peter asked his mother.

“No I shouldn’t think so. You know what he is like when his pride is hurt. Frank just wants everyone to do what he wants, and when he gets it wrong he thinks people are trying to be clever with him. Come here and give me a hug,” she said. She hugged her boy and stroked his hair away from his hot forehead. “You don’t remember your father, do you?”

Peter shook his head a little sadly.

“Well, I think you are just a chip off the old block,” she said.

“What do you mean?” Peter asked, confused.

“I mean you are just like your father was. He was very laid back, and very calm all the time. He always kept a calm head, even when everything seemed to be going disastrously wrong,” she said.“There was one time when he was out with some of his friends, and someone tried to pick a fight with him. The man was drunk, and obviously a bit dim, but he kept on trying to badger your father into fighting with him. Your father just stood his ground, was very calm, and just refused to get angry. He always said, ‘what’s the point in forcing things to go the way you want them to? You don’t get there any faster.’ And you know what? The man soon got bored and went off to fight with someone else. He was a wise man, your father, and I think you will grow up to be just like him. He always said that you should always be like water.”

“What does that mean?” Peter asked.

“Well, that nothing in the world is softer and weaker than water, but for attacking the hard rocks of life, there is nothing like it. It can forge through rocks like a knife though cheese. Look at the valley out there; that was all created by water once upon a time. It can wear away the earth, and cut through wood or stone, and yet when you dip your hand into the cool river, it feels like the softest, weakest thing in the world. So the weak always overcomes the strong, and the soft always overcomes the hard, in the end. And it is always better to drift where the current takes you, instead of trying to paddle your way upstream in your tiny canoe, battling against the force of something that has found its way through solid rock over thousands of years. But poor old Frank hasn’t worked that one out yet, so he keeps butting his head against everything trying to force his way through. Don’t you worry about a thing my sweet,” she said. “Frank will soon come round. You just try and keep being just like water, and it will serve you well in life.”

Peter pondered her words for a moment, and then pondered them a bit more, and went to find his favourite place underneath the willow tree by the side of the river, where the water gurgled and tumbled its way over the rocks on its endless journey towards the sea.

"Nothing in the world is softer and weaker than water, but for attacking the hard, the unyielding, nothing can surpass it. There is nothing like it.

The weak overcomes the strong,

The soft surpasses the hard,

In all the world there is no one that does not know this, but no one can master this practice.

Therefore the master remains serene in the presence of sorrow.

Evil cannot enter his heart

Because he has given up helping, he is people's greatest help.

True words

Appear paradoxical."

The 78th Verse of the Tao Te Ching by Lao Tzu

Howard Carter and the Donkey

Many years ago, when your Great Grandmother was just a little girl, a man called Howard Carter left England behind him to travel far away to a land of shifting sands in search of adventure. Carter went seeking the treasure of the pharaohs, and in particular, the last burial place of a little known boy king who, it had been said, was buried with much gold.

Three thousand years ago, when the Pharaohs still ruled in the land of Ancient Egypt, the people believed that after death you would go on a long journey, and travel through many perilous realms in order to reach the afterlife, where you would live happily for the rest of eternity. The pharaohs would spend most of their reign building great tombs for themselves, and have them decorated with beautiful paintings, and magic spells that were written onto the walls of the tombs. Then they filled them with pile upon pile of gold and silver and precious stones, and rather than being dank and dark places, the tombs were beautiful, and glittering and full of colour.

Sadly, because of the lure of the gold, robbers often broke into the tombs and stole all the treasure; so much of it was lost. By the time that Howard Carter stood in the Valley of the Kings, mopping his brow in the intense heat of an October morning in 1922, many of the tombs had been found already, empty and broken and damaged by the robbers. But Carter had been told the legend of a boy king whose tomb had not yet been found; who it was thought had been buried with much wealth. It was thought that because he was so young and he had died so suddenly, the boy king had been placed in a makeshift tomb, instead of the one that his architects had not yet finished, and no one had known where it was. Over the years people forgot he was there, and so he had remained undisturbed for centuries.

Carter had spent years searching the Valley of the Kings in search of the boy; in fact, he had been coming to the valley year after year since 1914, interrupted only by the war that raged across Europe. This was now the fifth year in succession he had come since the end of the war and painstakingly worked his way around the deep valley that stood beneath a great natural pyramid of rock. Month after month and day after day Carter tried, and failed to find the last resting place of the boy king. And each week he would send his telegrams to Lord Carnarvon, again telling him that they had not discovered young King Tut yet.

This season was bleaker than ever before. As usual he had planned to travel back to the West Bank of the Nile, but this time Lord Carnarvon had told him it would be his last trip. Dissatisfied with his lack of progress, Carnarvon had decided he would no longer be able to continue to fund Carter's search. So time was ticking away, and would soon run out.

Carter impatiently took out his pocket watch, and sighed heavily. He looked around himself once more, at the bleak golden-brown sheer sides of the valley. There was not a single bit of vegetation here, the lush banks of the Nile were a little way off to the east, and consequently the walls of the valley were clothed only in the desert sand which wrapped itself around either side of the green delta, stretching its arms out towards the rest of Africa.

Carter had had one certainty in his heart from the earliest days when he had first heard about Tut: that he would be the person to discover the tomb, and make his mark in the world of Archaeology. But five years in to the expedition and with time running through his fingers faster than the sand beneath his feet would have done, his self-belief was shaken, and his feelings of frustration grew with each passing unsuccessful day. He walked over to the shaded area where the water jar stood, and asked the boy sitting next to it for some water.

"Maya, minfadlak," he said, speaking in the boy's native Arabic.

The boy passed Carter a cup of water, which he drained, and turned his attention back to the area where his men were digging in the sandy soil, and even they seemed frustrated this morning. Tempers were short, and angry words had been traded more than once. Tomorrow would be the first of November. Soon their funding would be gone, and he knew he would have to return to London empty handed, to become the laughing stock of the Archaeological Society, or even worse, the person people all looked at with pity.

"There goes old Howard Carter," they would whisper behind his back, "as mad as a bag of snakes. Do you know he spent five years digging in the Valley of the Kings and still came back empty handed..."

Carter asked the boy for more water, dipped his clean handkerchief in it, and then took off his hat and wiped the back of his neck with the cool water and made his way back to the trench where he could see another argument was about to break out.

Later that evening Carter went back to his house, which sat a few metres away from the entrance to the Valley of the Kings. He was surrounded by his work; he ate, slept and breathed it, from the moment he arrived in Luxor to the moment he would leave at the end of the digging season. He sat on the little terrace, drinking a glass of mint tea, and he pondered his problem. He just couldn't see a solution at all. For five years now he had painstakingly worked his way up and down the valley, seemingly inch by inch, but he had not yet found the tomb. He was running out of places to dig, as well as money. He fanned his face with his hat, and sat staring at the mountain at the head of the valley, with its natural pyramid on top. That was why the Pharaohs had chosen this spot; the sign of Aton's pyramid led them here, and the virtually impenetrable valley walls protected them and the narrow, isolated valley, or so they thought. If they could have seen into the future they may have chosen somewhere else, but Carter at least was grateful they had not. Carter sat and just closed his eyes for a moment, enjoying the quiet.

That night as he lay in his little bed, his mind still battled with how he could find the tomb. Was there a single stone he had left unturned? A single area of the valley he had not already looked? If there was, he could not think of it. He got up and paced around the room for a while, still lost in his thoughts, and then looked out of the bedroom window. Away in the darkness he could see the fire around which the men who guarded the dig site sat, trading stories into the night as they shared a meal and the warmth of the fire. Even though it was hot in the day, the night could get very cold.

That night Carter was plagued by nightmares. His dreams were strange and he could not understand them, but he knew he was frightened. He dreamed of a serpent striking out to bite him, and he was running to try and escape it. But the faster he ran, the closer it got to him. He saw the group of men sitting round the fire up ahead, and shouted out to them to help him, but they just stood up, looked his way and started to laugh at him. Pointing at him and laughing. As the laughter reached a crescendo, he sat bolt upright in his bed, panting from his nocturnal running. It took him a moment to realise he was still in his bed, and that he had been dreaming.

The first of November dawned bright and sunny as usual. The sky was a clear intense blue, and the air was beginning to get warm, even though the sun had only just risen over the Nile Delta. Carter found he had no appetite for breakfast, much to the surprise of his house staff, as his mind was still too occupied with the problem at hand. His frustration was leaking out of every pore, and the men round him began to look away each time they saw him approaching, afraid to meet his eye in case he lost his temper and shouted, or worse. The day was again fruitless, and the night was again plagued by nightmares.

This time, Carter dreamed he was walking down Bond Street in London, which was bustling and busy with people. Up ahead, Carter could see a large crowd building around something, but he could not see what they were all looking at. As he approached he began to hear single words coming out of the crowd. They were gathered around a paper seller, who was calling out the headlines that day.

"Read all about it," the man shouted. "Howard Carter fails again! Five years and he still can't find the tomb!"

Carter felt his face turn a deep hot red, as he realised with embarrassment what was happening, but too late to avoid walking within a hair's breadth of the crowd. Suddenly, the paper seller spotted him, and pointed,

"There he is! That's Howard Carter! Look, his face is on the front page!"

The crowd turned to look, and seeing him a laugh rose from one of the people. And then another, and another, and soon the whole crowd was laughing hysterically at him, pointing and holding their sides because they were laughing so hard it hurt them.

Again, Carter sat bolt upright in bed, his face dripping with sweat. He was too disturbed to try and sleep again that night, and so he sat at his desk, writing in his journal and wondering what was to become of him. He had failed, he knew it. He just had to find a way of letting Lord Carnarvon know. He would have to pack up the expedition, send all the men home and then return to England. Perhaps he could avoid London for a while, and go and stay somewhere remote until people had forgotten about him. How long would it take for them to forget about his failure, one year? Ten?

By the time the sun began to climb its way over the horizon, Carter was exhausted. He knew he looked haggard and he almost didn't care; the dark circles under his eyes would betray his sleeplessness and his unshaven face would show the world the state of his inner mind. And he didn't even care this morning. He slowly walked up the valley towards the trench, all the while having an inner dialogue with the universe.

"Alright, you win. I give up. I will go home and forget I ever wanted to find this tomb, and you can just lie undisturbed for all eternity. You win. It is what you wanted, wasn't it? For me to give in and go home? Well now you will get what you want."

He stood overlooking the trench that day, knowing they would find nothing. By two o'clock he gave up and went back to his house, not caring any more about anything. He sat in his small bedroom, staring into space and just feeling the sense of silence grow around him. That night he slept poorly again, dreaming of being trapped in a darkened room where only a ghostly laugh kept him company. He could not tell where the laugh came from, as it seemed to echo all around him. He tried to hold his hands over his ears, but somehow that just seemed to make the laughing all the more loud. As the sun rose into the sky the next morning, Carter could barely drag himself out of the bed. He dressed, and glanced at himself in the mirror. His shoulders had drooped, his face again looked haggard.

He surrendered. Somehow seeing his face in the mirror made something inside of him give in and surrender to the flow of whatever would come to him now. He could no longer fight it. All he could do now was stop trying to paddle against the current. Little King Tut would remain undisturbed and Carter would return to England, older and hopefully wiser. But if he was to be laughed at, something in him knew he had to face up to his fears, and do it with a level of dignity. That morning he shaved, dressed in a clean suit, ate some breakfast and then made his way up the little dirt road to the valley where the men waited for him.

He tried to keep his spirits up that day, smiling at the people around him and praising them for their unrelenting hard work, and inside he knew he would miss them all when he left.

That night he went to bed early as usual, and this time was determined he would get a good night's sleep. He knew dreams could not hurt him, and neither could people's ridicule. If he just kept his own sense of dignity, all would be well. He knew he had to have faith that everything would be fine; it was just as it should be. He lay on his bed and waited for sleep to come and embrace him.

In the early hours of the morning, something woke him again, but this time it wasn't the nightmares that had plagued him for days. It was the sound of someone outside, running down the road shouting,

"Ya maar! Ya maar!"

The shouting got louder as the man approached the house, and Carter got out of bed. His Arabic was by no means fluent, but he at least understood some rudimentary words. Donkey? Why would a man come running down the road shouting about a donkey? He had no time to wonder however, as the man started banging on the front door of the house.

Carter got dressed and left the house, following the man who seemed excited but also a little scared. They walked quickly up the road, where just to one side of where they had been digging that week, a donkey had got its legs caught in a hole in the ground. The men were just pulling the donkey out of the hole, and it was braying loudly, distressed and dismayed at its predicament which had taken it by surprise.The men pulled the donkey away from the hole in the ground and Carter walked over to examine it. Even in the faint light thrown from the men's camp fire, the hole looked to be quite deep. No wonder the donkey had got stuck.

Carter called for a flashlight or a lantern, and one of the men brought a torch over and shone it in the hole. He gave a shout of surprise, and passed the torch to Carter.Carter shone the torch into the hole, wondering what the darkness would reveal. To his surprise, he could see a series of steps leading down. He could definitely see stone inside, and not the bare limestone one would expect to see in a natural cave or hole in the ground. It was a tomb. It was a tomb!

You see, although Carter had tried everything he knew, and used all of his powers of logic and deduction to try and discover the location of the tomb, the donkey, whilst minding its own business, had simply stumbled into a hole in the ground, and what did he find there? The steps leading down to the entrance to the lost tomb of the boy king, Tutankhamen. You see often, however hard you try sometimes you have to stop fighting, let the stillness form around you, and let nature run its course. If you are willing to look from a different angle, you may find the answer you are seeking has been there all the time.

But what most people don't realise when they read about the famous Howard Carter and his great discovery of the tomb of Tutankhamen in the Valley of the Kings, is that it took a donkey to show Howard Carter the way. You see the answers can come from the most unlikely of places, if you can just be open minded enough to let them come to you.

"By letting it go it all gets done.

The world is won by those who let it go.

But when you try and try,

The world is beyond the winning."

Ch 48, the Tao Te Ching by Lao Tzu

The Wood Imps' Holiday

There was once a small Wood Imp who lived with her friend in a little house in the woods. The Wood Imp was known to all her friends as Scout, because she loved to explore the woods and beyond where they lived, and would often go for long walks to explore the surrounding countryside, and in search of adventures.

Scout's sister was called Henrietta, and you couldn't ever imagine meeting two Wood Imps that were more different than each other (as I am sure you can imagine meeting two Wood Imps.)

Henrietta loved to do everything the "proper" way. Each time she had to do something she had not done before, she liked to consult the great tome of Wood Imp lore, which was called 'How To Do Anything A Wood Imp Should Ever Want To Do In Thirteen Easy Steps, So That You Get It Right Each Time Without Any Of Those Irritating Failures To Slow You Down And Make Life Difficult' or the "Wood Imps' How To" for short.

Henrietta never liked to take chances on not knowing exactly the right way to do something, and sometimes even if another Wood Imp knew exactly how to do something (having done it many times before) Henrietta was not averse to showing them the correct way to do something anyway. This resulted in many groans, and many small hands slapping against foreheads when Henrietta got her "Wood Imps' How To" out and cleared her throat to prepare for a lengthy explanation about something the unfortunate Wood Imp set to receive it hadn't asked for.

In fact, Henrietta liked nothing more than to study the "Wood Imps' How To" for hours on end, so she didn't even have to look things up anymore when the opportunity arose.

Scout on the other hand enjoyed reading books for fun, ("For fun?" you might ask… Absolutely!) And she didn't like to tell people what to do unless they had asked for it. She knew that the best way for people to learn new things was for them to try it for themselves, and even to fail sometimes in the process, because that way when they learned the lesson, they really remembered it. And as for the 'right' way to do something, Scout firmly believed there was no 'right' way to do anything, as long as a Wood Imp did what actually worked.

As you may imagine, Scout and Henrietta were like chalk and cheese, and you would think their house would be a home of slamming doors and shouting voices raised in frustration, and it would have been except for one thing; Scout was the very picture of calm and patience when Henrietta tried to tell her how she should be doing something. Scout always very calmly listened and considered Henrietta's way, but if she did not think it would work for her, she did it her own way anyway.

One day Scout decided she would like to learn to drive a car (for Wood Imps and Elves can drive small cars if they want to, but only if they do not harm the environment, thus the car that Scout learned to drive was powered by fresh air and magic). When Scout came home after her first lesson, she was very excited and was looking forward to telling Henrietta all about it.

"Did the instructor follow the thirteen easy steps as laid out in the "Wood Imps' How To"?" asked Henrietta, unable to contain herself.

"I don't think so," said Scout, "She didn't seem to need a 'How To' manual at all."

"How can you teach someone to drive without the "Wood Imps' How To"?" asked Henrietta, shocked and dismayed that anyone would even attempt such a thing.

"Well, easily I should say," said Scout, "as my instructor has been teaching people how to drive for a very long time, so I would think she knows everything a Wood Imp would want to know on the subject."

"Nonsense!" said Henrietta, "I've never heard anything more ridiculous in my life!"

On another occasion, Scout decided to go to Wood Imp School to take a class in how to identify and look after rare trees in the wood. Henrietta dismissed the whole thing as a ridiculous waste of time.

"But I am enjoying Wood Imp School," said Scout. "I get to meet lots of other Imps, and our teacher is very knowledgeable."

"I should think your teacher is very stupid," said Henrietta. "He would do much better to tell you to read the "Wood Imps' How To" and save your money."

Scout sighed, and changed the subject.

One year, Henrietta and Scout decided to go on holiday together.

"Where shall we go?" asked Scout, one morning after breakfast. "Shall we explore somewhere in this country or shall we go overseas?"

"Well, according to the "Wood Imps' How To" we are much more likely to catch a nasty illness if we go abroad. Perhaps we should just stay at home?" said Henrietta.

"Where is the fun in that?" groaned Scout. "Come on, Hen, let's have an adventure!"

"Ok," said Henrietta, reluctantly. "But if we must go, we should consult the 'How To' in order to find the right way to select a destination. I am sure the check list is on page one hundred and thirty seven, paragraph two."

"I have a much better idea," said Scout. "I went to Wood Imp Travel yesterday, and picked up some brochures. Here, look, she said, bringing out a big pile of glossy and colourful brochures. "How about India, or Europe, or Africa? Which would you prefer? I quite fancy South America."

"South America?" said Henrietta, "Why on earth would you want to go all that way?"

"Because it has the rainforest, silly!" said Scout. "What Wood Imp wouldn't want to visit the rainforest?"

"Well, they don't mention the rainforest in the "Wood Imps' How To"" said Henrietta, frantically leafing through the pages, trying to find it. "So perhaps we should go somewhere else? Look, it does talk about Imp's Regis, or the Imp River Valley. Or even Wood Imp World." Henrietta tried to show the pages to Scout, in an attempt at getting her interested, but Scout was determined she wanted to have a real adventure.

"No, I say let's go and have a proper trip to somewhere different, and if it doesn't appear in the silly "Wood Imps' How To", then all the better, I say!"

For once, Scout was insistent, and Henrietta realised that if she wanted to go away with Scout, she would have to brace herself for rather more of an adventure than she was used to. In the end, they decided on doing a tour of Greece, and planned to take in many historical sites on their journey. As they packed their suitcase, Scout packed what she thought she might need, while Henrietta packed what the 'How To' told her she would need, and of course she made very sure she packed her copy of the "Wood Imps' How To" in her suitcase.

On the day they were to travel, they made their way to the airport to catch their bird that would take them South towards the warm blue of the Mediterranean and their holiday destination. They were due to spend their first week on a lovely little island just off the mainland, and Scout was very much looking forward to the flight. She had flown by bird before, and she knew she was in for an exhilarating ride. As they arrived at the take-off point, she saw with glee that they were due to be flying by swallow, as the weather was getting cooler now and it was time for all the swallows to fly south. In fact, there were quite a few fairy-folk flying by swallow that day, so they all queued up and handed their suitcases to the staff-imps who were loading up the birds with the cases. On they climbed, and then the bird took off with a whoosh and a shout of joy from Scout, and a howl of alarm from Henrietta who was quite taken by surprise at the sudden rush of air.

Things went very well until part way through their journey, when the swallow that was carrying them did an unexpected loop-the-loop through the sky. Unfortunately, Henrietta's suitcase was not quite tied on properly, and just as the bird came upright again, Henrietta saw with dismay that her suitcase was plummeting down to the ground below. Henrietta grabbed Scout's arm and pointed.

“Oh dear,” said Scout, “You will just have to share my clothes with me!” realising that it was too late to ask the bird to land and look for the suitcase, as the suitcase was now very far away, and she didn’t speak bird language anyway.

“Oh dear,” said Henrietta. “Never mind all my clothes, what about my copy of the “Wood Imps’ How To”?” and she turned as pale as a ghost in shock.

Scout tried to put on her most sympathetic expression, but inside she could help smiling, just a little.

“Well, you will just have to learn what life is like without the rule book,” she said to Henrietta.

“Without the ‘How To’? I can’t do that! The only way I could know what to do without the ‘How To’ would be to read the section in the book which tells you what to do if you are ever without ‘the How To’, but I never read that part. I always thought I would keep it with me at all times.” At this point, Henrietta started to cry.

“Oh dear, never mind,” said Scout. “Life can be fun without the ‘How To’ book and it won’t hurt you, you know. Look at me, I don’t have a copy of it and I am just fine without it.”

But Henrietta would not be comforted.

After a few more hours of travelling, they landed on the island, and decided to go and have a good look round. At first they went to look at an ancient fairy settlement that dated back five thousand years. Scout enjoyed soaking up the atmosphere of the place, while Henrietta seemed a little pre-occupied and very tense.

“What’s wrong, Hen?” asked Scout. “Are you still worrying about your book?”

“Yes,” said Henrietta, a little sadly. “I was wondering what the facts are about this site, and what I would need to now about it.”

“What you would need to know about it?” asked Scout in surprise. “Couldn’t you think about how the place makes you feel instead?”

“Feel?” said Henrietta with a puzzled expression on her face. “It’s not all about me, you know. It is good for a Wood Imp to know what she should look at when visiting a site of historical interest.”

“Why not just look at what you want to look at, or what you find interesting instead? Go on, Hen, I dare you! Go with the flow, let your hair down and fly by the seat of your trousers just for once!”

“Well I never!” said Henrietta with a gasp.

But over the next few minutes, out of the corner of her eye, Scout could see something different happening. Henrietta was shivering slightly, as if there was something strange going on inside her body, and she kept getting a slightly glazed expression on her face, as if all the pathways in her brain were shifting around, and this was taking her attention away from the island.

Later on they went for dinner in a taverna that was built in a very old olive tree that had the most fascinating gnarled old trunk either of them had ever seen. As they sat down at their table and looked at the menu, Henrietta again looked a little overwhelmed.

"How can I know what to order when I don't have my list of 'Thirteen Things Every Wood Imp Should Try Eating When on Holiday on a Greek Island'?" said Henrietta with a frown.

"Why don't you just try eating what you feel like?" asked Scout.

"What I feel like?" asked Henrietta in bewilderment.

"Yes, feel. Or what sounds nice on the menu, or what you like the look of, you know, that is how the rest of us choose."

"Really?" said Henrietta. "I don't remember what that was like."

Just then, a waiter-imp walked by carrying a plate of steaming Kleftico, and Henrietta was suddenly distracted by the smell.

"Ooh, that smells lovely!" she said. "And it looks nice too."

"So why don't you try that?" said Scout.

Henrietta enjoyed her dinner that evening, far more than she had for a long time now that she wasn't analysing its nutritional content, or how much fat per gram on average food like this would contain. The taverna was a lovely place, with little fairy lights strung through the branches, and lots of interesting Wood Imps and fairy folk to watch.

The next day, they travelled high into the mountains to visit a ruined village that had been destroyed by a terrible earthquake many years before. After the earthquake, the villagers had left the mountains and moved down to the sea, but the old was still there. It was surrounded by olive groves, and the air was fragrant with mountain herbs. As they looked around what was left of the old buildings, some of the village still looked as if it had been left just a short time before; the old olive press was still sitting I the centre of the village, and the old village meeting hall was still standing. But as they walked further up the mountain slopes, they found more had been destroyed. At the top of the mountain slope, the church was no longer standing, and all that was left was a beautiful tiled floor that looked like a rug that had been shaken badly so that it rippled across the ground. Henrietta and Scout both stared in amazement at it.

"What would you do in an earthquake, Scout?" asked Henrietta.

"I don't know," said Scout. "It must have been so frightening for the people here. What would you do?"

"I was just thinking, that even the "Wood Imps' How To" doesn't say what you should do in the event of an earthquake, or any other big disasters. I think I would have been petrified."

"Absolutely," said Scout. "But I think there are some things that happen in life that no rule book can ever prepare us for. In fact, no 'How To' book could ever cover every possibility. I suppose that is why it is good to trust your own instincts, and your own judgement, because sometimes in life, that might be all you have to rely on."

"Hmm," said Henrietta, deep in thought. "Maybe you are right, and maybe, coming on this holiday and losing my suitcase was the best thing that has ever happened to me!"

"Really?" said Scout, beaming.

"Yes," said Henrietta. "It is making me forget the "Wood Imps' How To" and think for myself. This is fun," she grinned. "Just think, I can do what I want to, when I want to, without having to check the book for instructions. Yipppeee!"

Scout laughed as Henrietta did a little dance of glee.

So the Wood Imps continued their holiday, and had the best time ever. And do you know? Henrietta never again mentioned the "Wood Imps' How To" and they continued to have lots of exciting adventures together. And the next time they went on holiday together, they visited the great rainforest in South America.

"Living plants are flexible

In death they become dry and brittle

Therefore stubborn people are disciples of death but

Flexible people are disciples of life."

Verse 76, The Tao Te Ching, by Lao Tzu

"I hear and I forget. I see and I remember. I do and I understand."

Confucius, Chinese Philosopher and contemporary of Lao Tzu

Archie and Henry

There was once a very naughty boy called Archie, who lived with his dad in a small village in the middle of nowhere. Archie's dad was a farmer, and they didn't have much money, so Archie had to help his dad out on the farm whenever he came home from school. I wasn't that Archie meant to be naughty, but somehow adventures always found him, and somehow he always managed to land himself in scrapes and trouble.

Archie was quite a lazy little boy, so if he could find a short cut anywhere, or a quicker way to do anything, he would try, and this was what often led him into trouble.

If his dad asked him to tidy his room, instead of picking up all the things on the floor, he would simply push them under his bed, and one day when his dad asked him to clean out the hen house, his dad later discovered that Archie had simply left all the old straw in the hen house and simply covered it over with a layer of fresh straw. Stinky-poo!

Needless to say, Archie's dad was not very impressed whenever he discovered the results of an Archie shortcut, and he would tell Archie off and then make him do the task again. Of course this meant the task would take Archie three times as long to complete, as it would have doe if he had done it properly the first time round, but somehow Archie just couldn't help himself.

One day Archie's dad sent him to the village shop to get some groceries. It was quite a long walk to the village, but Archie always enjoyed the walk as the countryside was beautiful, and he liked seeing the other villagers going about their daily lives. Just as he was walking back down the road towards the farm, a car stopped on the road just ahead of him. A passenger in the back seat opened the back door, and threw something out onto the grass verge by the side of the road, then slammed the door shut, and the car sped off. Archie wondered what it was they had thrown out, and why they were in such a hurry, so he made his way over to the spot to investigate.

As he approached, he could see a small brown and white animal, sitting on the grass, shivering in fright. It was a puppy! Archie immediately picked up the poor little dog and stroked its fur. It looked dirty, and it hadn't been cared for properly, so Archie picked up the groceries in one hand, and held the puppy in his other arm, and made his way back down the lane to the farmhouse.

Archie suspected that if he told his dad about the puppy, he would make him find a new home for it. Archie had once asked for a puppy, and his dad had said no, (partly because the conversation came hot on the heels of one of Archie's particularly naughty shortcuts.) Dad said that Archie would never look after a puppy properly, and it wouldn't be fair. So Archie made the decision to keep the dog a secret. He had read about a girl who had kept a dog secret from her parents once, how hard could it be? His dad rarely came into his bedroom, so he could easily hide the dog there, and then he could sneak food in to feed it. As his dad was up early and out of the house tending the animals, Archie thought he would be able to hide the puppy in his schoolbag to get him out of the house, and then once they were out of sight, he could let him out to run.

'It will be lovely,' thought Archie. "I shall call him Henry, and we will be the best of friends!'

Archie took Henry into the house, dropped the groceries on the kitchen table and took Henry upstairs.

"First of all, you need a bath," said Archie to Henry. "You smell awful!"

So he bathed Henry, brushed all the tangles carefully out of his fur, and settled Henry into his room.

That night, Henry whimpered and cried, afraid of his new home, and unsettled b what had happened to him. Archie tried to comfort him and eventually tucked Henry into his bed to give him reassurance. The next morning over breakfast, Archie's dad asked him if he had slept well.

"Yes, fine, thanks," said Archie. "Why do you ask?"

"Oh, I thought I heard you whimpering in the night, and I thought you might have been upset. But when I looked in you looked like you were sleeping."

"Oh no, I was fine," said Archie, feeling distinctly uncomfortable. "I must have been having a bad dream."

Archie and Henry continued to go about their routine without detection. The school holidays would be coming in a week's time, so Archie knew he and Henry would have lots of time together then. For now, he would need to leave Henry in his bedroom with some food and water during the day, as he couldn't take him to school and he didn't want to leave him alone outside somewhere.

'It will be easy,' thought Archie, but in his confidence he had overlooked one very important detail. Henry, as most dogs are, was quite an energetic little thing, and when he was left on his own, he got bored very quickly, and when he got bored, he had a tendency to be very naughty indeed! In fact, as Archie would soon realise, Henry was just about the naughtiest dog he would ever meet.

On the first couple of days when Archie came back from school, everything was fine, but by the third day when he came home, Henry had been very bored ad very naughty. When Archie opened his bedroom door, he gasped in surprise. The room looked like a small tornado had been trapped inside (and in truth, one had been.) Henry had made his way round the room, systematically chewing through anything he could find that was chewable. All of Archie's plastic pens had been destroyed, and there was paper all over the room showing signs of tooth and claw marks. Even the bed was a mess, as Henry looked as if he had been there digging. And right in the middle of the floor, draped across one of Archie's slippers, was a great big doggy-poop!

In the midst of all this destruction, Henry sat, wagging his tail at Archie, as if to say, 'Look what I have done for you. Aren't I clever?' Archie groaned, dealt with the stinky dog-poo and decided he should take Henry out for a walk before Dad finished work.

They walked through the fields and played a game of 'fetch the stick' before Henry's little legs were worn out, and they headed back to the house. Archie's dad was in the kitchen, making them some dinner, so Archie rushed upstairs to put Henry back in the bedroom and then washed his hands and made his way down for dinner.

As they ate, the tension at the dinner table was very noticeable, and Archie wondered if his dad had seen the state of his room. It didn't take him long to find out.

"Archie, I went to your room to look for you earlier, and when I did I was absolutely horrified! How can you be that messy? Really, it is not good enough. You will need to clean it up before you go to bed. There will be no television for you tonight. You are really very naughty!"

Later that evening, Aunty Ginny from the village popped by with an enormous chocolate cake for Archie and his dad, it was really lovely. He liked Aunty Ginny and always enjoyed her visits, and he found his dad was always a lot more relaxed and happy when Aunty Ginny was there too. Once he had cleaned up the mess upstairs, Archie came down and had chocolate cake with Aunty Ginny and Dad.

The next day, Archie went to school as normal, and spent most of the day worrying about what Henry might be up to at home. When school finished, he rushed home as quickly as he could and was absolutely horrified when he got there. Somehow, Henry had managed to get out of the bedroom and then found his way down the stairs and into the kitchen, where he had eaten what was left of the chocolate cake (which was quite a lot) and then been sick on the floor. As Archie came in, he found Henry wagging his tail mournfully as he sat on the kitchen floor, obviously feeling very sorry for himself.

Archie realised he would have to move very fast to clear things up, so he picked up Henry, who was covered in chocolate as he had obviously rolled in some of it, and took him upstairs, intending to come straight down and clear up fast before his dad came in.

But just as he made it back to the kitchen, the back door opened and in walked Dad, to find Archie, covered in chocolate, standing next to the sick, looking very guilty indeed. Dad immediately assumed the obvious; that Archie had come home from school and gorged himself on the rest of the cake, and had then been sick on the floor. He was understandably very angry with Archie, who was then sent to his room in disgrace.

The next day was the last day of school, and Archie again worried about what he would find when he came home, but at least he had the comfort of knowing that it would be the summer holidays after today, and Henry wouldn't have to be on his own anymore.

Again, he rushed home from school as fast as he could and held his breath as he pushed open the back door. He was in for the biggest shock yet. There at the kitchen table sat his dad, with Henry on his lap.

"Hello Archie," said Dad. "Did you have a good day at school?" Archie nodded, wondering why his Dad was not shouting, and thinking this must mean he really was in big trouble now. "And who is this?" asked Dad, stroking Henry's head.

"Huh huh Henry," stammered Archie. "I found him by the road. Someone threw him out of a car and then just drove off."

"And when were you intending to tell me he was here?" asked Dad, but seeing Archie staring down at his feet with a very red face, he added, "Or were you intending to not tell me at all?"

"Archie, nodded, and mumbled, "I thought you would tell me I had to find him a new home."

"And did you think you would manage to keep him a secret forever?" asked Dad. Archie nodded. "That was a bit daft, son. Isn't that a bit daft, Henry?" he said, ruffling the top of Henry's head.

Henry wagged his tail and licked Dad's hand. Archie watched in surprise as he hadn't anticipated that his dad might actually like Henry.

"So what would you have done when Henry got bigger? You know it would have been a lot harder to hide him, you now. The reason I found him now was that he was sitting I your room barking to be let out. What would you have done when he got bigger and needed more food and more exercise? It is not fair to keep a dog shut up, you know."

"I know, sorry," said Archie. "I thought I would put him in my schoolbag when I needed to take him out."

"In your school bag?" Dad asked, with a laugh. "Henry will be a big dog, you know, when he has grown. He won't fit into your school bag for very long, and I would like to see you try and fit him in there when he has grown a bit!"

"Oh," said Archie.

"Don't you think it would have got harder and harder to hide him as he got bigger?" Archie nodded. He knew his dad was right. "I suppose there is one good thing," said Dad.

"What's that?" asked Archie.

"Well at least now I know it wasn't you who wrecked your room and was sick on the kitchen floor."

Dad started to laugh, and Archie started to let himself hope for the first time that maybe he would be allowed to keep Henry, if he asked.

"Dad," said Archie, "Can we keep him?"

Dad lifted up the puppy and held him in front of his face, so they were nose to nose.

"What do you think, Henry, do you want to stay?" Henry wagged his tail and Dad smiled. "But, Archie, you will have to look after him properly – no more shortcuts and no more trouble!"

"Ok," said Archie, taking his newfound responsibility very seriously.

And so Henry stayed, and became a loyal friend to them both Archie and his dad; when Archie was at school, he followed Dad around the farm, and when Archie came home, they would play together. Henry did indeed grow up to be a very big dog, and Archie would often feel relieved that he hadn't had to keep him secret all that time.

But one thing never changed; Henry was always the naughtiest dog you could imagine.

"Deal with difficult tasks while they are easy,

Act on large issues while they are small."

Verse 63 of the Tao Te Ching, by Lao Tzu

www.ingramcontent.com/pod-product-compliance
Ingram Content Group UK Ltd.
Pitfield, Milton Keynes, MK11 3LW, UK
UKHW020239250726
13967UKWH00001B/447

9 781291 169836